THE

KINGDOM

BLUEPRINT

From the beginning, God had a plan

CHARLENE RAMIREZ

PublishAmerica
Baltimore

First printing

PublishAmerica has allowed this work to remain exactly as the author intended, verbatim, without editorial input.

Hardcover 978-1-4512-8607-6
Softcover 978-1-4512-8608-3
PUBLISHED BY PUBLISHAMERICA, LLLP
www.publishamerica.com
Baltimore

Printed in the United States of America

I wish to thank my husband, Sergio Ramirez, my partner and my friend, who encouraged me, stood by me, and believed the Lord was leading me as a minister and as a writer. Thanks Honey.

I also wish to thank my dear friend and sister in the Lord, Veda Adams, who helped and encouraged me; thanks for taking the time to read, correct and encourage me.

I want to dedicate this book to my mother, Ellen Davis, for all her faithful support, and to my father, Charles Davis, who is at home in God's Kingdom.

PREFACE

In writing this book, I asked myself what was the purpose of writing a book about God. There are so many excellent books on this subject, and above all, we have God's word, the Bible. Did I really think I needed to write another book about God? Did I think I might have something to say that has not already been said? So what was my motive for writing this book? First of all, I would not have attempted it had I not felt led by the Spirit of God to do so. I felt compelled, inspired, to write a book not for the purpose of expressing some new thought or revelation, or to prove some point, but for the purpose of allowing God's Spirit to reveal more of God's heart.

The inspiration for this book came while I was praying one day about the Lord's return. I thought about the scripture at the very end of the Bible that states, "even so come quickly Lord Jesus". I thought on the passion of John's words, inspired by the revelation he had just experienced, as he wrote these final lines. It was written in the form of a prayer or plea, with such

5

anticipation, a deep yearning desire for the Lord to return. I thought about my own feelings at the moment, feeling the same overwhelming emotion, the desire to see Jesus. Suddenly, I felt the Spirit of God ask me a question, "Is this how my people feel?" I can't honestly answer "yes" to that question. Even though this is how we are supposed to feel, in truth, we don't see this kind of excitement and anticipation about the Lord's return among people. We are not seeing preparation for this event with any sense of urgency. Do people really believe he is going to return any time soon? Is the church busy about their Father's business, spreading the 'good news'? Are we preparing for his return? Unfortunately, the answers to these questions are not overwhelmingly 'yes'.

I began to consider the reasons as to why people are in no apparent hurry for Jesus to return. For one, they are too caught up in the cares of this world, enjoying all that this life has to offer, to seriously think about the Lord's return. Perhaps they have not taken the time to think about it, or maybe they don't have a clear understanding of what his return means. Many equate his return with the 'end' of things, which isn't a pleasant thought. In all reality, his return for us is the 'beginning' of things, of better things, of abundant life, full of joy, of love and of great promise. We don't anticipate or desire his return the way we should, because we still find things on this earth tolerable, even desirable, so we are not in any hurry for things to change. We have failed to understand God's heart, his will, and we are much more involved with accomplishing our own will than his.

This book began with the inspiration from the Lord to reveal, refresh, infuse, and inspire people to become passionate about his return. I believe God wants us to know more about his Kingdom, so we will feel more at home in the Kingdom of God. In order to understand his Kingdom, we have to understand his heart. It is my hope that reading this book will truly help many to understand and echo what John stated, "Come quickly, Lord Jesus".

*Scripture references used in *The Kingdom Blueprint* that are listed as KJV are from the King James Version or New King James Version of the Bible. Those listed as NIV are from the New International Version of the Bible.

CHAPTER ONE
THE HEART OF GOD

"I AM that I AM" Exodus 3:14

How do we as mortals understand the concept of an eternal God? Who is God, where did he come from, and what does he want with us? These are just some of the questions that mankind has been asking since the beginning of time. Volumes of books have been written on this subject. People have gone on quests, sought out holy men, waged wars, and gone to the ends of the earth searching for the answers to these questions. All that he wanted us to know concerning who he is has been documented in the most widely read and translated book of all times, the Bible. He is described as all powerful, all present, all knowing, which always is and always was. He is an eternal being, creator of all that was made; he has no beginning and no end. *"I am the Alpha and Omega, the beginning and the ending saith the Lord, which is, and which was, and which is to come, the Almighty." (Revelation 1:8 KJV)*

When Moses asked God who he was, God simply replied, "I AM that I AM", in other words, "I just am". Obviously, God did not see need for any further description, or the explanation was beyond man's ability to comprehend. He just is, and that is all we need to know! After all, this is a difficult concept for us as humans to understand, conceiving something that has no beginning or end. Almost every child has asked, "who made God?" The greatest philosophers of all times have not been able to answer that question. Though we cannot see God, everything that he has created testifies to his existence. *"For the invisible things of him from the creation of the world are clearly seen, being understood by the things that are made, even his eternal power and Godhead; so that they are without excuse."* *(Romans 1:20 KJV)*

God's creation is his testament to his existence. While man has concocted some theories as to the explanation for all which exists, that we simply 'evolved', or the universe was formed by some 'accident', the grandeur of creation itself testifies to the majesty of an almighty being, a creator who intelligently designed and created it. The more scientists learn, the more it confirms God's existence. Recently there was a scientist on a television program who stated what convinced him of the existence of God was research on DNA. He stated the more they researched DNA, the more complex it's design became evident. It is a master blueprint, which every living thing contains, detailing the specific uniqueness of every living thing. He stated, regardless of how, or if we 'evolved', the complexities of DNA proves there was intelligent design behind everything that was made, and it could not have possibly happened by accident. Intelligent design means somebody planned it all out. When we think of how no two fingerprints are alike, no two leaves or snowflakes are identical, no two individuals carry the identical DNA, and then multiply that by all the people who have ever existed, or all the snowflakes that have ever fallen, all the leaves, all the grains of sand, suddenly it becomes mind boggling; the intelligence that designed all this must be so far beyond our ability to comprehend. No wonder he just gave the explanation, "I Am that I Am". How could he possibly explain himself to man?

There is an account recorded in the book of Job where Job and his friends discuss the reason for all of his troubles. At the end of considerable debate, God finally speaks to clear up the matter. Although the Bible doesn't state whose hand actually penned the book of Job, which is considered to be the oldest book in the Bible, the eloquence of God's response to Job could only have been made by God himself. *"Where were you when I laid the foundations of the earth? Tell me, if you understand. Who marked off its dimensions? Surely, you know! Who stretched a measuring line across it? On what were its footings set, or who laid its cornerstone, while the morning stars sang together, and all the angels shouted for joy? Who shut up the sea behind doors, when it burst forth from the womb, when I made the clouds its garment and wrapped it in thick darkness, when I fixed limits for it and set its doors and bars in place, when I said, "This far you come, and no farther; here is where your proud waves halt"? Have you given orders to the morning, or shown the dawn its place, that it might take the earth by the edges and shake the wicked out of it? (Job 38:4-12 NIV)*

It's amazing how this account shows God's questioning of man's arrogance. Those who think they are wise and have all the answers are small and foolish compared to God, which is evident as God continues his discourse: *"Have you journeyed to the springs of the sea or walked in the recesses of the deep? Have the gates of death been shown to you? Have you seen the gates of the shadow of death? Have you comprehended the vast expanses of the earth? Tell me, if you know all this. What is the way to the abode of light? And where does darkness reside? Can you take them to their places? Do you know the paths to their dwellings? Surely you know, for you were already born! You have lived so many years! (Job 38:16-21 NIV)* In this statement, we can almost see God mocking man's arrogance, in a way that only the one who truly has all the answers could do. He questions mans ability to understand or control his own environment, much less the vast expanse of the universe: *"Can you bind the beautiful Pleiades? Can you loose the cords of Orion? Can you bring forth the constellations in their seasons or lead out the Bear with its cubs? Do you know the laws of the heavens? Can you set up God's dominion over the earth? Can you raise your voice to the clouds, and cover yourself with a flood of water? Do you send the lightning bolts on their way? Do they report to you, here we are? (Job 38:31-35 NIV)* If we stop to think about the depth of God's questions to Job, we realize that he is asking Job, "Who are you to question me? Do you know how my creation operates? Well, I do!"

In studying the book of Genesis, we see God made the light and the darkness, then he divided them and created lights to hang in the heavens. I viewed a program about the universe; the size of our universe is beyond our comprehension. The heat of one star is intolerable for anything to abide, and yet God formed them, and "hung" them in space! I can just imagine him taking a handful of stars and hanging them in the heavens, like hanging ornaments on a Christmas tree! Who could possibly do such a thing? Imagine for a moment the size of our universe, who could create such dimensions? When we think of the greatness of God, sometimes we forget who he really is.

When we contemplate how he made a living being, with a heart that beats, lungs that filter air, a circulatory system that feeds blood to the entire body, a nervous system that relates impulses back to a brain that operates all of these functions, and then realize this all functions without man's understanding or control, even while he is sleeping! Not to mention that upon waking, we can converse, learn, multi-task, while our body continues to operate, without us giving a thought to it. How is it that someone with very limited intelligence can still operate on such a complicated level, without his understanding of the process? Think for a moment of ancient man, without the scientific knowledge of how his body works, and yet his body functioned regardless of his ability to understand it all. Obviously, there was a designer who made us to operate so efficiently, regardless of the level of our own intelligence. How could someone say there is no God? There is so much definite evidence that an intelligent design was behind creation.

When I begin to think of the greatness of God, and his majesty, and then think that someone so marvelous would care so deeply for us as individuals, it moves me to tears. Jesus said that the very hairs of our head are numbered and known by God. Can you imagine that? Every little detail, every molecule of our being, he is intimately aware of. When we think of all the people there are, and how many have ever lived, we start to get a glimpse into the greatness of God and his love for mankind.

What we don't know about God is enormous, and it will take us all eternity to comprehend, but one thing he has revealed to us about himself is his profound love. The Bible, in its simplicity, was given to man to give us an insight into who he is, and what he created us to be. It begins in Genesis by saying, "In the beginning, God created…" and then simply states that he created the heavens and the earth, light and dark, without too much detail as to how, for the common man would not have understood if he had given a great detailed account. What he does reveal is his purpose in making all this, and whom he made it for, by the statement, "let us make man in our own image". Though God refers to himself in plural, it does not mean there is more than one God, but rather, it is an insight into his nature, revealing the depths of his personality. The Bible refers to God as being 'one God'. The scripture tells us that Jesus was there at the beginning, and that all that was made, was made by him. *"In the beginning was the Word, and the Word was with God, and the Word was God. He was with God in the beginning. Through him all things were made; without him nothing was made that has been made. In him was life, and that life was the light of men. The light shines in the darkness, but the darkness has not understood it." (John 1:1-5 NIV)*

God is a multi-dimensional being, having different personality aspects, as does his creation, man. We are body, soul and spirit, having different dimensions as well. We, however, are not capable of separating ourselves into three parts where each part can exist somewhat separate or independent of the other. Our body is our living quarters, our soul is our personality where our thoughts and feelings are, where our heart abides, and our spirit is the very essence of life, a living spirit that continues to exist once the body or 'house' dies. We can't separate our mind or our emotions from our body, for we are dependent upon our body to be able to feel and to think. We can't separate our spirit from our body, for if we do, our body dies. We are totally dependent upon these three working together as one in order to continue to live. God is able to separate and still fully exist and still be 'one'. The best example I have heard, which explains the Trinity, is in the simple example of an egg. We can take an egg and break it, separating the white from the yoke, and then use the white in one recipe, the yolk in another, and place the shell still in yet another place. All three parts of the egg are being used differently, yet they are not three different eggs, just one, which carries the unique DNA of that oneness. This is one very simple explanation of a being that is so far beyond our ability to comprehend, for his depths and dimensions of 'being' are far beyond our comprehension, but it does give us a little insight into understanding the nature of God.

What God wants man to understand about his nature is seen in the human manifestation he has revealed to us in Jesus. To understand the heart of God, all we have to do is look at Jesus. God took his heart and put it in human flesh; his name is Jesus. All that we need to know about who he is, and what he is like, is seen in Jesus, revealed through what he said and did. He stated that everything he did was what he saw his Father do, and everything he spoke was what his Father told him to speak. He said he was one with the Father, and when asked to reveal the Father, he replied, "If you have seen me, you have seen the Father." Jesus is God's image to man, the revelation of his heart, the mediator, the physical communication of who God is, so that we might understand God and be able to respond to him. Our ability to reach out to God, or be more like him, as we were created to be, is impossible for us to accomplish by our own merits. We could not reach up to him, so he reached down to us by becoming one of us. What a marvelous testimony to his great love for us! To understand who God is, we only have to look at the one he sent, Jesus.

We often think of him as a meek little baby lying in a manger, yet this meek baby was the essence of God in human form. He is the same God who "is, and was, and shall be"; the one who formed the earth, who created the heavens, and hung the stars in space; the creator who made all things, and by him all things continue to exist. He is the only one who can answer all of the questions posed in the book of Job. He knows the measurements of the universe, he knows the depths of the sea, and lightning bolts answer to him. When I pause to meditate on these things, an overwhelming feeling comes over me. I am so in awe of God and his greatness, that words can't express it. There is such an excitement in my being to be loved by such a creator; what a marvel to have the privilege to worship him, to know him, and the hope of spending eternity in his presence.

We have just scratched the surface as to who God is, a subject that will take all of eternity to discover, if it is possible to fathom even then. It amazes me that some have the concept that we will sit around in heaven playing harps, implying that it might become a bit boring. Nothing could be farther from the truth! Imagine all there is to learn! I imagine it won't be seated in a classroom, or from a book, but a show-and-tell of sorts, where God will actually let us see how he made everything. He might even teach us how to create things! Can you imagine that? Since he wants us to be like him, it is plausible to think that he would teach us to do the things that he does as well. They say that man only uses about 5% of his brain capacity. What is the other 95% for? Perhaps we will find out the answer in eternity.

I can't imagine why people don't believe in God, why wouldn't you want to believe in him? God created mankind with such purpose, with such care, so that he might be able to share himself and all of his mysteries with us. Why would you create something so marvelous, so complex, if it's potential was only a brief existence that ended rotting away in a box? What would be the purpose to all the effort, and to the great sacrifice of coming to earth to die for them, if they only lasted a few years, and then ceased to exist? In examining who God is, and his divine plan for mankind, life takes on meaning. It wasn't an accident, it wasn't random; it was designed by a Supreme creator, with much care and detail, but above all with an eternal purpose.

If we take the time to consider who he is through what he has chosen to reveal to us in Jesus Christ, we can comprehend a little more concerning him, and what is in his heart, and thus, have an even greater insight as to why he created us.

CHAPTER TWO
GOD'S PURPOSE IN CREATING MAN

"Let us make man in our image, after our likeness"...(Genesis 1:26)

To fully understand God's purpose for mankind, we have to review what he has said in reference to us. God is our Creator; the Bible documents his creative nature from the beginning, revealing his ability to create by speaking things into existence; he created light just by simply saying, "Let there be light". Many speculate as to the origins of earth, but God tells us that he "spoke" and it "was". Although many find this incomprehensible, and far too simplistic, God is God, why couldn't he have done it? It is amazing to realize that before he created everything, he planned it all in his mind first, and then he spoke it into existence. Like a master builder, he had a Kingdom blueprint in his mind first, and then he created all that is according to his blueprint.

The Bible says that he created day and night, the sun, the stars, and the planets, but it appears that he created planet earth with a purpose and design different from his other celestial creations. He created this planet to sustain life; he gave it a breathable atmosphere; he created seas and dry land on the earth. He made animals of all kinds, and he created the trees and grass that would produce food to sustain them. What was the purpose in creating all of this? Was it like some big canvas, and he was in the mood to "paint" a pretty picture? It was far more than that.

When a woman is about to have a child, she begins to plan way before the baby arrives to assure everything is ready for the blessed event. She wants everything prepared for the baby's needs, for his warmth and comfort. In much the same way, God was preparing the earth for such a blessed event. He was getting ready to create man. He was going to create a child that would be just like him, in his image and likeness. He wanted to create someone whom he could love; someone he could communicate with; someone he could "raise" and teach all the wonderful things of his kingdom to. He wanted a family! The Bible states that "God is love", and 'love' needs something to love in order for there to be fulfillment. God's heart desired children which he could love.

God created us to be in his likeness, in his image, with a purpose. The makeup of man from a human standpoint was taken from the physical elements or chemicals found in the dust of the ground. But the creation of the spirit of man was taken from the spiritual realm, from God himself. He is a triune being, Father, Son and Holy Spirit. We are also a three-part being, body, soul and spirit. Only man is described as having a living soul, "a spirit being", a gift received from God, which makes him God's 'offspring', a true 'son' of God. *"And the Lord God formed man of the dust of the ground, and breathed into his nostrils the breath of life; and man became a living soul." (Genesis 2:7 KJV)*

God created a physical being that was also a spiritual being, one capable of understanding him and living forever with him. He created us as complex beings, with physical aspects and needs, as well as emotional and intellectual needs, but above all, our spirit has spiritual needs. The spirit in man searches for its creator. It searches for meaning, for truth, to know, 'why am I here?' It is a gift to every man, a beacon, a 'homing device', that propels us to seek after God. Man can fill his belly and satisfy his physical needs, but something is still missing in his existence. He can reach the highest levels of intellect, and still something eats at him, something still remains empty and unfulfilled, a hole exists deep inside him. The need for something more drives him to search, to explore. It is the spirit within us searching to be reunited with our creator. Only spiritual things can fill this need, and only by connecting to our creator, our heavenly Father, can we fill the need in our spirit. God made us this way so we would need him and feel incomplete without him. We can only reach a sense of purpose and total fulfillment in our life when we turn to him, when we come 'home' to God. He wants us to know his heart and to receive his love.

Just as God has the ability to create things, he gave us creative ability as well. He has authority over all he has created, and in teaching us to be like him, he gave us authority as well, but on a much smaller scale. He gave us something to exercise authority over, in order to train us to be like him. *"And let them have dominion over the fish of the sea, and over the fowl of the air, and over the cattle, and over all the earth, and over every creeping thing that creepeth upon the earth." (Genesis 1:26 KJV)* God made a safe environment for man, a warm, pleasant place that provided everything man would need to survive and flourish. He had created all the animals so man would have something to care for, something to exercise dominion over. In order to teach his children valuable lessons, such as love, sacrifice, and responsibility, he gave them pets to care for. We often get pets for our children for the same reason, to teach them responsibility as well as to give them something to love and play with.

It can be seen in the light of the Bible, that the earth was created for man. God gave man authority over the earth, and over everything which was on the earth. He had to give man the ability to have authority over something, if we were ever to be like him and be able to understand his nature. We had to have experiences and abilities in common in order to better understand and relate to our Father, our creator. He gave us the ability to have children, and to feel parental love, so that we might get an insight into his heart and his love for us.

It's interesting here to note what God did on the 7th day. *"And on the seventh day God ended his work which he had done, and he rested on the seventh day from all his work which he had done."* (*Genesis 2:2 KJV*) He took the day off! He stopped creating and took the day off to enjoy his creation. He wanted to spend time enjoying his new family. His purpose in creating everything, all the preparations for the 'big day' were now complete, and now he could enjoy his children. He spent the seventh day allowing them to draw close to him and know him. This was exactly what he had wanted, to create children to love, with the freedom of will to choose to love him in return.

Chapter two of Genesis, appears to reiterate the events of God's creation, giving more details concerning the creation of

Adam and Eve than in chapter one. This is where we see the utmost care in preparing the earth, and specifically, a garden home to place man where the vegetation would sustain him. He even provided for a mist to water the garden; there were no storms to harm his children or the agriculture that sustained them. He considered every detail in providing a perfect, safe, ecological environment for his children. Genesis 2:4-14 details this account. Such care went into the plan, such devotion; how is it that mankind can't understand the heart which did all this?

God gave Adam responsibilities, as well as rules. He wanted Adam to grow, to use his skills and gifts to develop into a mature man, much as any parent would, but he also let Adam know even though he had authority over his environment, he was still responsible to a higher authority than himself. *"Then the Lord God took the man and put him in the Garden of Eden to tend and keep it. And the Lord God commanded the man saying, "Of every tree of the garden you may freely eat; but of the tree of the knowledge of good and evil you shall not eat, for in the day that you eat of it you shall surely die." (Genesis 2:15-17 KJV)*

One of the jobs God gave Adam was to name all the animals. *"..And he brought them to Adam to see what he would call them. And whatever Adam called each living creature that was its name." (Genesis 2:19 KJV)* What an experience that must have been! It was probably quite amusing for God to watch the reaction his new child was having at seeing all the different types of animals, and imagining names to call them all. Some of the names he came up with might have been quite funny sounding, but undoubtedly God was amused. It brings to my mind when my children were small and first learning to talk.

What a joy! You could listen for hours with such delight as they tried to pronounce things. Granted, Adam was not a baby, but he was God's child, and I am certain that God was enjoying every minute with his new creation. God delights himself in his children.

All this must have kept Adam very busy and quite entertained for a long time. But I imagine as he saw every animal had its female counter-part, how they would stay together, and curl up together to sleep, a sense of loneliness, a feeling something was missing must have become evident not only to Adam, but to God. Adam had all these 'toys', but he wasn't a boy, he was a man. He was growing and beginning to demonstrate the need for having someone else, like himself, as a companion. He needed someone to talk with and share all these new experiences with. He had God with him, but as every parent knows, there comes a time when a child grows and needs other types of relationships. They need someone they can care for, someone to share things with, but most of all, someone to love. The desire to create a family comes from God; it is part of his nature. This nature is what caused God to make man in the first place. As Adam was growing in God's likeness, this need became apparent in him as well, the need to have someone to share his love with, and together create new life. *"But for Adam there was not found a helper meet (suitable) to him."* (Genesis 2:20 KJV) God knew this would happen. He had already made a plan to meet this need; *"And the Lord God said, "It is not good that man should be alone; I will make him a helper meet (suitable) for him."* (Genesis 2:18 KJV)

As a parent, there is such a delight, such a sense of love and awe when you hold your newborn baby. You didn't know it was possible for you to love so deeply, so unselfishly. The joy of becoming a parent is indescribable. As the child grows and takes his first steps, he does the cutest things, the laughter and happiness he brings far outweighs the work involved. Watching your children grow and develop as human beings, with their own distinctiveness, and every now and then, catching a glimpse of yourself in one of them, brings such a sense of satisfaction, of accomplishment. They are your world, and you are theirs. But the day comes when this isn't enough for them anymore; they start to display the same needs that once drove you to find your own way. The day comes when they launch out on their own and seek to find someone with whom they can start their own family. Some parents try to hold on to their children, to postpone the inevitable, finding it too difficult to let go, but true love knows you can't be happy if the one you love so much is unhappy. It is a great joy as a parent when your child finds that special someone and falls in love. You have memories of the wonderful feeling of falling in love and you rejoice that your child is now experiencing it. They are no longer little children, no longer dependent on you for everything, but now, as adults, they are able to understand and relate to you on a new, different, more mature level. They are suddenly able to totally give of themselves to another. Their world becomes less self centered, and the nature of self sacrifice for the well being of another becomes more evident.

This is the reason God created a mate for Adam, not only to bring him joy, but so he would continue to grow in the likeness of God. It was God's plan from the beginning to make male and female, giving us the ability to reproduce after our own likeness. He wants us to experience those same feelings, those same responsibilities. He wants to raise us in "his image and his likeness". There is nothing more life changing to teach you the depths of love and of responsibility like becoming a parent. It gives you an insight into the heart of God and the depths of love he has for us. When I became a parent, my understanding of God's love, and my appreciation of his love grew enormously. The heart of the Father was more perfectly revealed to me through the love I felt as a parent towards my child. My relationship and understanding of God took a much turn towards a much deeper, devoted relationship. This is not to say that those who don't have children can't comprehend God's heart, but for me, it gave me a personal insight that revolutionized my faith.

The Bible states God caused a deep sleep to fall over Adam, and removed one of his ribs, and used it to create a woman, of the same make up and design as man, but much different. He created someone who would compliment man, someone who would be a helper, a companion and friend, and the mother of his children. I have heard statements about the weakness of Eve, concerning how she was tempted and then, in turn, convinced Adam to disobey God. Women for centuries have been seen as lesser, or inferior in the mind of some, but we know God created her to be the perfect mate for Adam. Some might question, why did God make her so sensitive, so gullible? God wanted someone who was capable of loving his son to a deep degree, someone with sensitivity and understanding, capable of giving of herself, who would be an encourager, a friend. God took great care in making Eve to be just right for Adam. Eve was not made in haste, or in error. The sensitivity that she needed to be his help mate was her strength, but also her weakness. Her naïveté and curiosity were that of a child. She had not grown up with a human mother to teach her, nor did Adam. Everything was new for both of them. The devil took advantage of their naiveté, their innocence, and their desire to learn, in order to deceive them, and she was the most vulnerable. In our nature as human beings there is a great potential for good, but there is also the potential to doubt, to question, to be deceived, and to disobey. This is what free will is all about, the ability to make choices. God gave us this ability so that we could freely make the choice to love him and serve him. If he had created us to be pre-programmed to choose only what he wanted for us, then freedom of choice would not exist. God created us to be free as he is, with the right to think and choose, as he does, in other words, to be in his likeness.

After God had created man and woman, it states: *"And God blessed them, and God said to them, be fruitful and multiply, and replenish the earth, and subdue it." (Genesis 1:27-28 KJV)* He commanded that they be *"one flesh" (Genesis 2:23)*. He wanted a family! He instituted the family unit; it was his creation! He wanted them to use the authority he had given them to govern over the earth, and he wanted them to use the love he had given them to love each other and create new life. God's plan was seen by him as good, *"And God saw everything that he had made and behold, it was very good." (Genesis 1:31 KJV)* He could have just created other children himself, but he wanted to share the joy of that experience, the experience of becoming a parent, with us. He wanted us to know his joy!

God gave man one condition to all this, obedience. In essence, God was saying, you may be like me, you may have been given my love, my authority, my nature, but you are not over me, or equal to me. You must remember who created you. I am still greater than you are, and you must obey me! The symbol of that obedience was the tree of the knowledge of good and evil. Man at this point was pure and innocent, and did not yet have the concept of evil. God stated the punishment of disobedience up-front, nothing hidden, by stating the consequences of disobeying him: *"but you must not eat of the tree of the knowledge of good and evil, for when you eat of it you will surely die."* *(Genesis 2:17 NIV)* God had told this to Adam before he created Eve, and most certainly Adam would have told Eve what God had commanded.

I can only imagine the surprise Adam must have had when God first brought Eve to him; imagine his delight, his insatiable need to take her by the hand and show her everything. He must have introduced her to all of his pets, and told her the name of them all. He would have given her different things to taste, but most certainly, he would have pointed out the tree of the knowledge of good and evil and told her that God had commanded them not to eat from that tree. Perhaps God himself told Eve, as he walked in the garden with her and Adam, and spent time with them. He must have been delighted having a new daughter. It must have brought God great joy seeing the happiness his gift had brought to Adam. As a parent, there is such a delight when you you're your child something which brings them such pure joy. I don't know who enjoys it more, the child receiving it, or the parent watching the expression on their child's face. God must have enjoyed the difference of a daughter, and seeing her unique reactions to everything. Surely God cherished every minute of it!

The amount of time that they spent in the garden before the day the serpent showed up to deceive her, is not known, but some time must have passed. When the serpent appears and speaks to Eve, the impression is she's alone at that moment. Perhaps the devil took advantage while Adam was tending to one of the animals or while he was sleeping to make his deceptive attack. However it occurred, the fall of Adam and Eve into sin would set them off on a different course than what God had originally intended for them, but then, God knew they would fall. From the beginning he already had designed the plan to redeem man.

CHAPTER THREE
MAN'S FALL

Why the fall? Didn't God know that this would happen? Of course he did, and he made provision for it in his Kingdom blueprint. He made us in his image to be like him, but with one stipulation, we remember who he is, and obey him. Even the laws which govern civilized societies are dependent upon obedience to the authority of the land. We were never to think of ourselves as supreme beings, or as gods, but as God's creation, his children, always under his authority. Growing in his likeness involves becoming aware of our potential, as well as exercising our right to make choices; it involves governing our own actions, and taking responsibility for those actions. Having power and using that power wisely are two very different things. Exercising power wisely involves understanding right from wrong and making wise, unselfish choices. This step in our growth process is a very dangerous one, but a very necessary one in order to become a responsible adult. Growth involves risk.

When our children become teenagers we try to guide them, while teaching them how to exercise their right to choose. We begin to give them more freedom to make choices, but we also outline consequences for when they disobey the rules and choose unwisely. It is part of the growth process to help them become mature, responsible adults. There are times when we lay down a rule for their own well being, which they will challenge. On occasion they will exercise their independence to choose, and defy us, and argue with us, until we get to the point of exasperation and state, "because I said so!" We draw a line and if they cross it there will be consequences. In essence, this is what God did, he created a line which they were not to step over or there would be consequences. When our children disobey, it often breaks our heart. We suffer as much as they do, if not more. I don't know any parent which enjoys having to discipline their child, but we do so because we love them, and ultimately, it is in their own best interest. Love involves responsibility, and the risk of heartbreak.

Why create the tree of the knowledge of good and evil? Why put this challenge before them? In order to grow up to be a responsible adult, you need to be aware of right and wrong in order to make the right choice. Being created in his image, we had to confront the reality of choice, and of our own free will, in order to determine what choice, or what road, we would choose. If there are no choices, if everything is pre-determined for us, then there is no growth of character. We can't grow into his likeness without confronting choice, which encountering the knowledge of good and evil. Adam and Eve already had the knowledge of good, for God is good and they knew him. He had told them not to eat of the tree of the knowledge of good and evil because he did not want them to fall away from him. What parent wants to see his child fall? You can tell them what you want them to do and what the consequences of disobedience will be, but you can't make the choice for them; they must make it for themselves. Growth involves choices.

Death seems like a pretty serious consequence doesn't it? God didn't start out with little consequences. "Death" means to be separated from "life". *"He is the life, the light of men."* *(John 1:4 KJV)* Death is being cast into outer darkness, or to be separated from the light. The choice to disobey God was a choice to see darkness, to see evil; they already could see what was good; God was right in front of them! The devil, in serpent form, "beguiled", or deceived them into choosing his side, the side of darkness, the side of evil. He used the cunning words of deception, *"has God said?"* *(Genesis 3:1)* He was questioning God's word, his authority, and in the process, he was teaching them it was alright to question God's authority and to rebel against him. The act of rebellion is when we question whether God knows what's best for us, or whether he has the right to dictate rules for us. It takes God off of the throne as the ultimate authority, and places our self on the throne, in essence, deposing God and making our self the supreme ruler or god. Our disobedience would separate us from him. I have heard countless stories of young people who rebel against their parents for one reason or another, and leave home to do things their own way. I have heard the heartbreak it causes their parents, especially when the outcome turns to tragedy. The heart of God wants to protect us from our own foolish choices that can be so destructive. We often can't see the reasoning behind the rules that he set for us, just as our children might not, but he expects us to trust his love and wisdom, knowing that everything he does is for our own good.

Lucifer, (Satan) was an angel of light before he rebelled against God: *"How you are fallen from heaven, o Lucifer, son of the morning! How you are cut down to the ground, you who weakened the nations! For you have said in your heart: I will ascend into heaven, I will exalt my throne above the stars of God; I will also sit on the mount of the congregation on the farthest sides of the north: I will ascend above the heights of the clouds. I will be like the Most High."* (Isaiah 14:12-14 KJV) Not only did he rebel, he led a host of angelic beings in the rebellion. Now he was teaching God's children to defy God's authority, and sowing seeds of doubt by stating what God had told them was a lie. *"You will not surely die", the serpent said to the woman, "for God knows that when you eat of it your eyes will be opened, and you will be like God, knowing good and evil."* (Genesis 3:4-5 NIV) He was working to erode Eve's trust in God, and he successfully managed to plant doubt in her heart: *"So when the woman saw the tree was good for food, and that it was pleasing to the eye, and also desirable for gaining wisdom, she took some and ate it."* (Genesis 3:6 NIV) I imagine she must have rationalized her disobedience (as we all have done). She may have thought, "God is good; who wouldn't want to be more like him, and if we eat from this tree, like the serpent said, we will become wise like God. She obviously convinced Adam it would be okay because it would be good to be wise like God. The Bible states they both disobeyed and ate the fruit.

I have heard different interpretations on this passage from a variety of ministers. One explanation I heard was that Adam ate the fruit Eve offered him because he did not want to risk being separated from her, regardless of the consequences. Adam knew if Eve disobeyed and was punished by death, he would lose her and be alone again. I have also heard some say that Adam was a fore-runner of Christ, and thus, was willing to take on the sin of Eve and to die for her, as a fore-shadow of what Christ would do for us one day. Whereas these opinions may have some merit, it's still just speculation, as the Biblical account does not include any more explanation as to why or the mind set of Adam at the moment. The Bible simply states that Eve took the fruit and gave it to Adam and they both ate. Regardless of whatever his motive to disobey was, he chose to listen to Eve over listening to God, making Eve more important at that point in his life than God. He gave in to her counsel and allowed her to be the ultimate authority over the destiny of their lives. Whatever his thoughts were, or his motive, he had been told directly by God, whom he had walked with and talked with, and knew intimately. He had a choice to make just as Eve did, and they both made the choice to disobey God.

Disobedience in essence means, "I know what's best for me, not God", or at the very least, "I know what God said, but that's not what I want to do." Haven't we all experienced this behavior at some point in our life? Haven't we seen this behavior in our children from time to time? The curiosity to explore the unknown, the thrill of risky behavior, and the self gratifying, 'devil may care attitude', are part of the human nature in all of us. God made man able to choose, intelligent, curious about life, with a desire to create, a desire to explore, but he also set boundaries that man continues to challenge and rebel against to this day.

Why such a severe sentence? Why not just a 'time out', or a lesser consequence than death? The consequence of going down the path of the knowledge of evil would cost Adam his soul, and not just his soul, but the souls of all humanity. The price to redeem them from the path of evil would be the highest price of all, the death of Jesus Christ on the cross. No wonder it was such a serious issue. Once man started down the path of the knowledge of good and evil there would be a great potential for good deeds, but also a great potential for evil deeds. It was something that could not be undone or taken back. It would, however, lead us to become more like God, in the aspect that we would have the knowledge of both, and the freedom of choice to choose. Unfortunately, we are not enough like him to make the right choice. He knew the consequences of giving us the freedom to choose, hence, his warning. Man's weakness and the devil's continual temptation would ultimately cause man to choose sin over righteousness, darkness over light, over and over again.

As a result of their sin, God sent Adam and Eve out of the Garden of Eden, and placed an angel to block them from eating from the tree of life. Can you imagine man, who chooses to do evil, living forever in such a state? The fear of death and judgment is the last restraint to keep man from doing more evil. Although not even the fear of death seems to restrain him, at the least it keeps him from perpetuating more and more evil by ending his life. Such great suffering man has inflicted on humanity. Thank God the potential of man to harm others is shortened by death; can you imagine the wickedness and destruction on earth if men like Hitler were immortal? While we often hear of the consequences of their sin, and what a bitter lesson it was for them, it is seldom mentioned the heartbreak it must have caused God, or the disappointment he would have felt.

God told Eve the consequences of her being deceived and for allowing herself to be used to deceive Adam. As a result she would experience sorrow and suffering in childbirth, and she would have to be subservient to her husband from then on. It seems clear this was not his original design for things. They were to be partners, equals, and friends. She was a gift from God to Adam, designed to be his help mate, his companion, to help him be all that God intended for him to be. She was a particular creation, made by God, with special gifts, attributes, and talents in order to fulfill a vital role in God's creation, and in Adams life.

For generations, many cultures have placed women as little more than servants or objects to be acquired. Some, in the name of religion, have furthered this concept, using scripture to control or to down play the importance of women in God's plan. Nothing could be further from the truth. The scripture states in the spirit there is neither male nor female but all are one in Christ. (Galatians 3:28). In other words, God doesn't love his sons more than his daughters. He does not think of woman as a lesser or inferior creation. He created woman with purpose; he delights in the uniqueness and difference of his creation. Women were made more sensitive, gentler, to complement and add to the fullness of his creation, and with the purpose to 'help' man. When God made us in his image, he poured attributes of his own nature into us. In men we see some distinctive characters, such as a protective nature, a provider instinct, while as in women we see others, like nurturing, gentleness, maternal devotion, to name a few; both are important and necessary in God's plan for humanity.

Jesus never treated women as lesser individuals, and it is a shame so many throughout the ages, including some religions, have done so. We can see the tenderness, the love and mercy which he showed, in the case of Mary Magdalene, or the Samaritan woman at the well. He never treated women as lesser beings. Being a woman is a gift, a privilege; it is an honor to be created to be a wife, a help-mate to man, and a mother who will nurture and raise future generations. It is no small task which he gave women, and it should be held in honorable regard.

God had made a beautiful world in which his children were meant to grow and learn. Originally, the ground produced everything they needed to survive. God had made it to be so in order to provide everything for his children. They were safe from harm; they could walk in the garden and talk to God; they could actually see him whenever they needed to. What a wondrous place that must have been! However, the punishment for their rebellion was separation from God, and from the place he had made as a home for them. They would have to provide for themselves, since they had rejected his provision by disobeying him, and had chosen to go their own way. Now they would have to work by the sweat of their brow in order to produce for themselves, and the ground would not always yield for them. They had abandoned God's plan, his provision. They had displayed a desire to be independent, to do things their own way. How many times did we fail to follow our parent's instructions? How many times did we think we knew better? Don't we hear that same thing from our own children as well? 'I know' is the phrase we often hear from them, before they plunge into making a wrong choice. We can attempt to guide them, but unfortunately we are often unable to make them understand our reasons, or listen to the plea of our heart.

The consequences of not listening to wise counsel and doing things on our own often turn out disastrous. As much as you desire to spare your children from heartache and tragedy, sometimes the only way to correct the rebellious, independent, destructive behavior in our own children is to let them pay the consequences of their actions. The consequences of Adam and Eve displaying they wanted to do things their own way was: they would have to make it on their own from then on. In none of this did God ever say, "I am abandoning you". God still continued to speak to his children, and to be there for them when they called out to him, as is evident in Genesis chapter 4 when he speaks to Cain. We never stop loving our own children, regardless of the mistakes them make. We don't abandon them, even when they disappoint us and break our heart. Why would we think God would do differently?

In order to walk in harmony with God, man has to choose that which is good, for God is good, but repeatedly mankind chooses evil, and in so doing turns their backs on God. God, on the other hand, has never given up on us, even when mankind came to a point that their wickedness was to such an extreme no good could be found in them. Still, God searched, and found one who still sought after him, who chose what was good over what was evil; that man was Noah. *"Noah found grace in the eyes of the Lord." (Genesis 6:8)* What a story of hope! What a testament to the love of God! He waited, he looked for a child who would turn and respond in a positive way to him.

God spoke to Noah, as he had to Adam, and he told him his plan to rid the earth of the wickedness of mankind. He told Noah to build an ark so he and his family, along with every species of animal, would be saved. God destroyed the evilness of man, but spared the one who freely chose to do that which was good, against all the influence to do the contrary. He wanted children to love, who would love him in return, and was not willing to abandon that quest.

God has always rewarded those who seek after him with their whole heart. Regardless of our imperfections, and the mistakes we make, God looks at our motive, the hidden intent of our heart. The person who reaches out in faith, who realizes his sin, his inadequacies, as well as his need of forgiveness and draws close to God, has always been precious to God. The Lord waited patiently for generations for such a man to seek for his friendship, not willing to give up on his plan or on his creation. And so God started all over again with Noah and his family. Unfortunately, the knowledge of good and evil abided in them as well, even though Noah chose good, some of his descendants did not follow after his example. Faced with the same choices, they did not make the choice to follow after God as Noah had. What a heart break for God this must have been. He once again had to endure the rejection of his creation, as mankind hardened their hearts against him once again. For again, sin prevailed and humanity set out on the path that spirals down; man went his sinful way and turned his back on God. In all this, God still stretched out his hand to mankind, and searched for one who would turn back to him, one who would chose the right path; this time it was Abraham.

Abraham hungered after a relationship with God. He chose to do what was right, to reject the evil of the times in which he lived, and to commit his way to God. He chose to believe, in a time that other's had chosen not to retain the knowledge of God in their hearts. Abraham looked for God, and he became God's friend. What a joy it must have been for God to have a child that wanted to be with him! He had waited so long, and at last, there was another one! Because of this, God entered into a covenant with Abraham, a holy promise, to bring a solution to the dilemma of sin, a sacrifice to pay for man's sin, the promise of a savior, a messiah. His covenant with Abraham was to give him and his wife, Sarah, a son. What was even more amazing is Sarah was barren, and they were both well beyond the age of childbearing. With God nothing is impossible! God told Abraham through his offspring all nations of the world would be blessed. He revealed he would use the lineage of Abraham to bring forth his own Son who would bring the ultimate solution for the reconciliation of man with God. Through the seed of Abraham, God would reveal his heart. He would come in the flesh to settle the issue of sin once and for all!

God fulfilled his promise and gave Abraham a son, which he named Isaac. When Isaac was a young lad, in a fore shadow of God's own future plan, God told Abraham to take Isaac to a high mountaintop where he was to sacrifice him. (God was revealing what he would do for us one day. He would send his son, and sacrifice him in order to redeem us and give us a chance to find our way back to him.) Though he did not make Abraham go through with sacrificing Isaac, the outcome would be different when it came time for him to sacrifice his own Son, Jesus. He fully intended from the beginning to resolve the issue of mans sin, by paying the price for their transgression with his own blood, a plan that once set in motion, he did not turn back from until it was finished. His determination to make us into his image and likeness, to set us free to reach our great potential has never changed. He was willing to make the ultimate sacrifice to achieve it, and he did so, on the cross.

What depths of love, what unconquerable faith, what great hope he has for his creation, his children! We were unable to choose obedience, to choose that which is good on our own, so he himself took on the form of a man, to buy us back from the curse, to pay the price that had to be paid in order to fulfill the sentence pronounced against us. HE CAME TO OUR RESCUE! He made a way through Jesus Christ for us to be adopted back into the family! Not only that, he wiped the slate clean! He forgave all our sins and gave us a brand new beginning, a "do-over". He sent his Spirit to inhabit us in order to give us the extra strength, the power, to choose the right thing and the power to overcome the temptation of the evil of darkness. This was the ultimate chance for man to start over again, by accepting his Son Jesus. It came with forgiveness, and with help to finally be able to achieve the goal of being able to walk with him and to grow in the light of his love. Fellowship was restored. God himself came in the flesh to show us how to walk. He set the example; he became the mediator, and he became the sacrifice, paying the penalty for our sins. What an amazing solution to the dilemma of mankind!

What we need to realize is God's plan and purpose for us has never changed. This is the reason for detailing the account of man from the beginning, for revisiting man's history, so that we might know God's plan for creating us. His desire for us has never changed. In his word he tells us: *"I am the Lord that changes not." (Malachi 3:6 KJV)*, and, *"Jesus Christ is the same yesterday, today, and forever." (Hebrews 13:8 KJV)* He created us for his pleasure; he created us with a purpose in mind. He created us to be like him so he could love us and share himself with us. He wants to be with us. He wants us to reach our fullest potential. He wants to provide for us, protect us, and give us his nature, his authority. He still wants us to be in "his likeness, and in his image".

The Word of God gives us prophetic signs, statements concerning the coming of his Son, our Messiah. He wanted his people to believe that he was going to come to their rescue. He was indeed going to provide a lamb, a sacrifice, to atone for their sins. He left clues through his word so his people would be able to identify their Messiah. He spoke through his word, telling them to take his word to heart, to cherish it, and pass it down from generation to generation. He wanted them to retain the knowledge of him, and to be able to recognize his provision, his Son, when he came.

I am certain there were those who searched the scriptures, waiting for a sign. Some waited their whole life, and did not see the promise fulfilled. Generations passed, and man became tired of waiting, tired of hoping, and returned to doing whatever seemed right in their own eyes. Still, there have always been those few who seek after God, those who don't try to fill the void with whatever the world offers, but cry out to God with a desire to know him.

CHAPTER FOUR
GOD'S SOLUTION

God's blueprint included the solution to man's dilemma. He knew from the beginning man would fail. Failure is the option of free will, of choice. But God included a provision in his Kingdom blueprint to cover our failure, and he, himself, would be a part of the blueprint, as the solution for the redemption of man. It brings to mind the painting by Michelangelo which depicts God stretching forth a finger towards fallen man, who has his hand outstretched towards God. God himself would reach out to us; his plan was to overcome our weakness in order to complete his design for man. His desire was to have us with him for eternity, regardless of the personal sacrifice he would have to make in order to fulfill his plan.

Jesus was sent to mankind as the greatest gift God would ever send, in a time referred to as 'the fullness of time'. It was a time when Rome had taken over much of the known world. Israel had gotten about as far away from the knowledge of the true living God as was possible, while still claiming to retain the knowledge of him. They followed rituals and traditions, but they had little real knowledge of who God was and what his plan or purpose was. Expecting him to come announced as a king with all the pomp and ceremony they were accustomed to seeing in earthly kings, they were completely taken back by the entrance of God's Son into the world.

He did not come in splendor or ceremony; he came as a small child born to a young, simple virgin. He was not born in a beautiful palace, but in a mere, humble, borrowed stable. He grew up as a common child, not appearing any different than any other child, but there was nothing common about him. He was wise and compassionate. Little is known about his early life on earth before he entered his public ministry, except for the fact that when he was twelve years old he traveled to Jerusalem with his family for the Passover feast. While he was there, he became separated from his earthly parents. They assumed he was with relatives, so they began their journey back home, only to discover that he was not with family as they had supposed. They returned back to Jerusalem to find him in the Temple speaking with the priests and leaders concerning the things of God. Distraught, they inquired why he had done so, to which he responded, "He was about his Father's business". Nothing more of much significance about his early life, his home or day to day family life is recorded.

His mission is all that seemed to matter. He came with a single purpose, to redeem us from sin and bring us back to the Father. He came to reveal God to us. Through accepting him, God's plan might be revealed to us and his nature might be manifested in us. He picked common men to follow him, not kings or rulers. He wanted us to understand that he loved all men, and he was not a respecter of persons. It also makes mention that there were women who followed him, as well as little children, and he showed great love and compassion towards them all. Jesus showed equality to all, at a time where women were treated with little respect, of little value, he demonstrated God's love equally to all. He had compassion on the masses, healing them and ministering the Word of God to them. He traveled about with no luxury or political ambition. He came to reveal the heart of God to mankind, and he did so through his great love for mankind. He embraced children and said theirs was the kingdom of God. He spoke a great deal about his Father's kingdom, a kingdom where pride and worldly worth or fame had little to do with. Yet many were not impressed by him. They wanted something grander, something revolutionary; they wanted someone who could overthrow the Roman Empire and establish the kingdom of Israel. Though he spoke the most important words ever recorded, and did the greatest miracles and signs, still many were unconvinced. He was not the messiah they wanted.

Those who followed him and heard his words, even his disciples didn't seem to fully understand who he was, or what God was about to do through him. And so, in fulfilling God's plan from the beginning, he was taken to a cross, where the world thought they would be rid of him, where the devil thought that God's plan would finally be defeated. There in the most unjust, heinous crime of all times, God's Son, Jesus Christ was crucified. Love was crucified, put to death for our sin, our rebellion. I imagine it was a day when all of heaven was in quiet sorrow and angels' tears fell silently down.

I cannot imagine a love so divine that no sacrifice would be too great. As a parent, I can appreciate, to some extent, the sacrifice our Heavenly Father made by giving his only Son for us. I could not willingly sacrifice one of my children in such a cruel way, especially for those who had deliberately rejected him, who were full of sin and hypocrisy. How he endured the cross, we will never fully understand, or be able to comprehend the depths of such a love. I can only imagine how the Father must have felt as he allowed his plan, his blueprint, to play out. Certainly, if there was another way, he would have found it, but there was no other way. The ultimate parental love, the ultimate loving sacrifice was made. The Lamb of God, the Son of God, was sacrificed for the sins of man, so that an eternal pardon could be established for us all. It is too wonderful for me to understand. All I can say is that I am so thankful, and will be forever grateful that Jesus looked down the halls of history and remembered me while he was on that cross, and my children, for had he not, we would all be without hope.

The story does not end there. When Jesus gave up the spirit and cried "it is finished", his blood sealed a new covenant. The redemption of all mankind was bought by the price of his blood. On the third day, the grave could no longer hold him; he came forth in what must have been the loudest roar of praise of all time in heaven. The tears of sorrow were transformed into shouts of victory and praise forevermore; like bells sounding throughout heaven, shouts of "worthy is the lamb!', "Our Lord is alive!", and "He reigns forever", must have echoed throughout the universe. He has paid for the forgiveness of all, and promised to those who believe in him, eternal life. Even as he is alive forever, so we too will live with him forever!

Jesus coming to earth, dying for our sins, WAS the plan of

God for the sinful condition of man from the very beginning. Jesus is the Messiah, the expected one, the lamb to be sacrificed. The Cross is the key to the kingdom of God. Without what Jesus did for us on the cross, there would be no way to be reconciled with our Father. There would be no place for us in God's Kingdom. Jesus is the key, whereby we can enter into eternal life. He is the very center, the heart of the Kingdom blueprint.

So Jesus came to establish God's Kingdom, and he fulfilled his mission on the cross. When he stated "it is finished", he was stating that everything which needed to be done in order to reconcile us with the Father, everything needed to fulfill God's law, his righteousness, was accomplished through his sacrifice on the Cross. The King was triumphant! His kingdom is now established in and through his children, who accept the Living King into their hearts and lives. Where the King is, his kingdom is. Now his kingdom can reign in the hearts of those who believe by faith in him. He establishes oneness with us, indwelling us, as was his desire from the beginning, to share our lives with us and have us participate in his kingdom as his children. The glorious Kingdom of God has begun in the hearts of all who believe in the King!

CHAPTER FIVE
THE STATE OF THE CHURCH

Once Jesus "finished" the plan for the redemption of man, the work of building the kingdom of God began. This work was delegated to the first born, his disciples; they were to build the Church. It is God's plan to use us to build his kingdom. He has a definite plan and a perfect will for his church. Jesus taught his disciples to pray, *"Thy kingdom come, thy will be done, on earth as it is in heaven." (Matthew 6:10 KJV)* It was part of God's plan from the beginning to establish his kingdom on this earth in the heart of his children. Though man's sin had separated him from God, it did not cause God to change his plan for creating us for his pleasure, or deter him from his goal to form us into his likeness. We rebelled; we turned away from him, but now, the door to reconciliation was wide open. Jesus opened the door for us to be able to be back in his presence. But not all mankind embraced God's way, in fact only a few came to the Light. It was entrusted to those who understood, those who chose to accept God's redemption plan, by accepting Jesus and his sacrifice, to take up the mission of carrying this good news to all men.

What about our weakness, and our sinful nature? How would we keep from giving into our fleshly nature and making the same mistakes over and over? Would we continue to be deceived as Adam and Eve had been? God had paid for our sins, the slate was clean, but how were we to walk successfully and not fall again? He included provision for our victory in his kingdom blueprint as well.

Jesus told the disciples to remain in Jerusalem and to wait for the promise from his Father. He told them: *"I will not leave you orphaned."* *(John14:18 KJV)* He gave them a reason for why he had to leave them: *"Nevertheless, it is expedient that I go away, for if I do not go away, the comforter will not come unto you; but if I go, I will send him unto you."* *(John 16:7 KJV)* He also said, *"When the Spirit of truth is come, he will guide you into all truth; for he will not speak of his own authority, but whatsoever he hears, that will he speak; and he will reveal to you things to come."* *(John 16:13 KJV)* God was making a provision against our weakness. There was definitely a plan at work, he would provide for us by sending his Holy Spirit to help us. Jesus had done his job, he had given his life, and he had paid the price. He showed us how to walk as God's children; we finally had an example to live by, but he was not going to leave us without help to succeed. He knew how frail we are, how weak we can be at times, he knew it first hand, for he had become flesh, and had lived among us. He experienced temptation; he was bombarded by the enemy; he knew what it was to feel physically weak. He was going to send us strength; he was going to leave us a teacher, a guide, a comforter, his Holy Spirit. If the enemy was overcoming us, he was going to give us someone to strengthen us and fight right alongside with our spirit. What a great, generous, loving God we have! He keeps fighting for us; he keeps on loving us, regardless of how often we have failed. We are his children, and he will not give up on us!

He gave his followers, the Church, a job to do, a mission to fulfill. We were made joint-heirs in his kingdom through adoption; *"For as many as are led by the Spirit of God, they are the sons of God. For ye have not received the spirit of bondage again to fear; but ye have received the Spirit of adoption, whereby we cry, Abba, Father. The Spirit itself bears witness with our spirit, that we are the children of God."* (Romans 8:14-16 KJV) We have been made children of God and partners in this endeavor. We are to proclaim God's plan to reconcile the world back to him through the sacrifice of his son Jesus Christ. We are to edify the church, to build each other up. We are to take the power he has given us through his Holy Spirit, and the tool of his word, and use it to teach God's ways to man. God uses his word to cleanse and transform our minds, so that we can change our negative, worldly ways of thinking, and begin to think as he wants us to think. We are to "think with his mind"; cleaning out all the junk and sin that clutters our minds and keeps us from becoming more like him.

The word of God empowers us against temptation. It is referred to as a "two-edged sword" with which we can defend ourselves against the onslaught of our enemy. It gives us the knowledge of good; it fills us with "the mind of Christ". *"For who has known the mind of the Lord, that he may instruct him? But we have the mind of Christ."* (I Corinthians 2:16 KJV) We are told to put on this new nature; *"But put on the Lord Jesus*

Christ, and make no provisions for the flesh, to fulfill the lusts thereof." *(Romans 13:14 KJV)* We are told to let God renew our sinful, degenerate way of thinking so that we can choose freely to do good, and in doing so, be changed into his image, his likeness. The word of God is the tool that he uses to get rid of what hinders us, and what he uses to empower us to achieve our greatest potential; *"And do not be conformed to this world, but be transformed by the renewing of your mind, that you might prove what is that good, and acceptable, and perfect will of God."* *(Romans 12:2 KJV)* God's word also tells us that he is taking all that is working against us, and using it to work to our advantage to form us into being like his Son. *"For we know that all things work together for good for those that love God, to those who are the called according to his purpose. For whom he did foreknow, he did predestinate to be conformed to the image of his Son, that he might be the firstborn among many brethren."* *(Romans 8:28-29 KJV)*

This is God's marvelous plan at work! Through the ages, he has stayed the course. I have quoted a great deal of scripture so far, in the attempt to prove, with God's own words, why his word is so important to the success of his goals for us. Our sinful nature, (a part of us because of the knowledge of evil), has "stacked the deck" in our enemy's favor, but God has given us a tool to overcome that nature. First of all, he evened the playing field by wiping the slate clean when he forgave our sins by sending Jesus to pay the price. Next, in order to give us a fighting chance, he gave us the strength of His Holy Spirit, and the instrument with which to defend ourselves. The Bible is the truth that stands against all the knowledge of evil. What of our right to choose? Does the word of God take away this right? In no way, but to the contrary, it enables us to be free from the evil influences so we are able to freely choose. The carnal mind is polluted with evil thoughts, concepts and images. God, by his Holy Spirit dwelling in us, uses his word to clean us up, to bring us back to a pure, clean, innocent way of thinking, so we are freely able to choose that which is good, which enables us to walk in obedience to God. The carnal mind is incapable of doing this on its own. We are not able to succeed without his help. Yes, he forgave us, he saved us, but unless he cleans us up and changes the way we think, we will fall again and again.

God wants us to succeed. Just look at the investment he has made in order to insure that we do. He won't violate our right to choose by making us into perfect little robots. He wants us to choose the right way. He wants to make us like him, free to be, free to choose, knowing good and evil, yet choosing freely to do that which is good. God is good, he chose to be good. God is love, he chooses to love without reservation, without conditions, and he created us to be like him. Mankind needed his help, and he came to our rescue once again, as he always has. He created a way back to him. He created a solution for our problem, and he himself gave us the tools, the help, and the strength to succeed. The sacrifice on the Cross, the gift of the Holy Spirit, the Word of God, all are his plan to get us back to where it all began, back to being created in his image and in his likeness.

Why has God gone to so much trouble? So we can live in fellowship with him and reach our fullest potential to live an abundant, joyful, victorious life. Isn't that what any father wants for his child? The Bible states: *"Beloved, now are we the sons of God, and it does not yet appear what we shall be, but we know that, when he shall appear, we shall be like him, for we shall see him as he is. And every man that has this hope in him purifies himself, even as he is pure (I John 3:2-3 KJV) this* is God's goal, his purpose for us.

Do we see this happening in the church of today? As decades pass, we see the church in its ups and downs. We see great times of renewal when God's people turn to him and seek him with their whole heart; we see great waves of repentance and revival, but we also see times of "cooling off". There have been times where the world seems to close in and the church departs from obediently following God in order to follow after the ways of the world. There are some victories and some defeats, but the church, although not defeated, is a far way from walking as a victorious church, a bride without spot or blemish. Worldliness often creeps in and the cares of this life over-crowd the hunger for God. In the book of Revelation, the Spirit of God warns the church of these things, and though it is words are before our eyes, the warnings often seem to go unheeded. The enemy refuses to give up the fight. He continues his onslaught. He continues to stack the deck against us. He draws us into the carnal realm, into the carnal mind, by bombarding us through every means he can, knowing full well what God has said in his word regarding this: *"For to be carnally minded is death, but to be spiritually minded is life and peace. For the carnal mind is enmity (at war) against God; for it is not subject to the law of God, neither indeed can be. So then they that are in the flesh cannot please God." (Romans 8:6-8 KJV)*

The devil is trying to defeat God's plan for us; he is trying to keep God from reaching his goal to transform us into his image, and unfortunately, he seems to win the battle sometimes. God's plan does not end with our defeat; it ends on a note of victory, with the promise of the return of Jesus Christ to overcome once and for all the enemy of God's children. He has given us the tools to overcome the enemy, but believers often don't use those tools. The scripture states, concerning the days before the return of Christ, there will be a falling away from the faith: *"Let no man deceive you by any means: for that day shall not come, except there come a falling away first, and that man of sin be revealed, the son of perdition;" (2 Thessalonians 2:3 KJV)* The Bible continues to say: *"Now the Spirit speaks expressly, that in the latter times some shall depart from the faith, giving heed to seducing spirits, and doctrines of devils;" (I Timothy 4:1 KJV)* There is a war going on against the Kingdom of God, and against the children of the King. The devil does not intend to let go of his vengeful plan against mankind easily. This is a war that has been going on throughout the ages. As it draws to a close, we can expect to see an intensified effort by the enemy and his forces to pro-long the outcome. Satan is fully aware of what God has said, and knows that his time to wreck havoc is drawing to a close. He knows the sentence that will be imposed against him for all of his rebellion and all the harm he has caused mankind. No wonder he is fighting with such intensity, trying to put off for as long as he can, the inevitable, total defeat. We are his target; harming us is his greatest goal. After all, what greater hurt can you cause someone than to harm their children? We are not pawns in this war; we are God's treasures, his children which he has spared no expense or sacrifice to defend. Jesus promised he would return, and he will! In the Gospel of Luke, Jesus speaks to his disciples, telling them of the need to always pray and not faint, by saying: *"And will not God bring about justice for his chosen ones, who cry out to him day and night? Will he keep putting them off? I tell you, he will see that they get justice, and quickly. However, when the Son of man comes, will he find faith on the earth?" (Luke 18:7-8 NIV)*

This scripture has troubled me for many years, and should concern all of those who serve God. Jesus questioned whether he would find faith when he returns. I don't believe that he did not know the answer concerning this. I believe this is more a question to provoke us into evaluating our faithfulness to God. Will we fall away, or will we persevere in faith? Will we put so much value on this life, on this world, that we allow the things of God to slowly be pushed away? This is what the enemy is trying to do, but this question is supposed to wake us up to the truth, by leading us to make the decision to fight back and say, 'NEVER!' We can never take our eyes off of the prize, which should be the goal set before us. We need to keep in mind our purpose for being created, and the great cost that was paid to achieve that goal. We are not speaking about the small, temporal life of this world; we are speaking about our existence in eternity. Why do we continue to live as if this lifetime is all that matters? We are so narrow-minded, and so easily deceived into believing this is all there is. God's plan, his design for us, is so much greater, if we can just catch a glimpse of it, and hold fast to it, life would take on a completely different meaning. We were meant to live forever with him! Jesus stated repeatedly that his purpose was to give us eternal life, he prepared a place for us in God's kingdom. *"In my Father's house are many mansions: if it were not so, I would have told you. I go to prepare a place for you. And if I go and prepare a place for you, I will come again, and receive you unto myself; that where I am, there ye may be also."* (John 14:2-3 KJV) We cannot question God's purpose or plan, nor the great price he was willing to pay in order to bring us back to him; *"For God so loved the world that he gave his only begotten Son, that whosoever believes in him should not perish, but have everlasting life."* (John 3:16

KJV) His word makes it completely and undeniably evident what his plan and motive is, love. God made a way to overthrow the sentence of death imposed by man's disobedience; Jesus said, *"Verily, verily, I say unto you, he that hears my word, and believes on him who sent me, has everlasting life, and shall not come into condemnation; but is passed from death unto life."* *(John 5:24 KJV)*

CHAPTER SIX
THE MYSTERY OF TIME

As previously stated, God's purpose is to form us into his image and likeness, but man, exercising his free will, took a wrong turn off of God's path. God set in motion a redemptive plan to restore us back to the pre-fall state, in order to get us back to where he created us to be. What completely amazes and humbles me is, he became the solution to man's dilemma, by becoming one of us. He paid for our sins, by canceling our debts, and served our sentence for us. The fall was made by choice, man's freedom of choice, so redemption was also made by choice, God's choice to save us. Since it was our choice to rebel, we now get the opportunity to choose whether to accept or reject God's pardon, by accepting Jesus Christ. Those who accept him, receive a pardon from their sins, for he paid the sentence. They must choose to now live their life for him, since he gave his life for them. Justice is fulfilled; the sentence was paid; he took our place, so we could go free. What a marvelous plan! It is so clear, so easy, almost too good to be true, and yet it is true. God is that good; it is beyond our ability to comprehend such love, such goodness, and such unselfish sacrifice.

The long wait for God's plan to come to its ultimate conclusion has brought about much speculation. Two thousand years have gone by, and the church is still waiting for his return, for the prophetic events foretold in the Bible to be fulfilled. Time may be a concern for us, but it is not an issue with God. What is two thousand years compared to eternity? The Bible states, *"But beloved, be not ignorant of this one thing, that one day is with the Lord as a thousand years, and a thousand years as one day."* (*II Peter 3:8 KJV*) Time is an earthly concept with earthly limitations. God literally has 'all the time in the world'. Still, many question why it has taken so long for the Lord to fulfill his promise to return. The word of God answers this question by stating: *"The Lord is not slow in keeping his promise, as some understand slowness. He is patient with you, not wanting anyone to perish, but everyone to come to repentance."* (*II Peter 3:9 NIV*) God is patiently waiting for mankind to hear the good news of his plan for salvation, waiting for man to make the choice. His perfect will is for everyone to accept the savior and thus, be reunited with him. This is totally understandable when we consider the depths of the love he has for mankind. Why wouldn't he prolong the days so the maximum amount of people can be spared? However, the word of God tells us he will not wait forever. What a tricky balance! His love constrains him to wait until the last moment, so more people can be saved, yet with each acceptance of his grace, there are more born who will ultimately reject him and not receive his salvation. Let us not forget the statement he made; "when the son of man returns will he find faith on the earth?' We know he desires everyone would choose salvation, but what value is there in waiting for the last few to enter in, if it endangers those you already have?

The Bible warns us there will be a falling away from the faith before his return. God set a certain date, known by only him, a specific day for the Lord's return. We can only speculate on how God chose that day. I am certain it was not a number or date picked at random, the "weight" of the world, the fate of mankind, had to be weighed in the balance. Jesus was asked the question concerning the coming of that day, to which he replied, *"No one knows that day or hour, not even the angels in heaven, or the Son, but only the Father."* *(Matthew 24:36NIV)* Men throughout the ages have claimed to have insight as to when the Lord will return. Some have come up with astounding theories as to how they reached the conclusion of what date it will be. Many have trusted in these so called prophets, and been deceived, having their faith crushed simply because they have not paid attention to what the Lord said when he stated, "no one knows that day or hour". While men love to think they have a revelation from God, which only they were given, to make themselves look somehow more spiritual, the truth is in the word of God, Jesus said no one knows! He did give us signs, or clues, but the exact date is not for us to know.

The key to understanding prophetic events is time itself. Without the 'key' or time element, prophecy remains a mystery; there is always an unknown part of the equation. It is like a giant puzzle, which God took and broke into pieces, hiding some of the pieces throughout the Bible. The first thing we have to do is locate these pieces, and then we can attempt to fit them together. It is hard to construct an accurate picture, when you are missing some of the pieces. It is equally as hard to reconstruct an image, when you don't have the picture of what it's supposed to look like in front of you. You may find some pieces that fit together, but you can't figure out if they are located at the bottom or top of the puzzle. If you have ever done a puzzle before, you know it is extremely difficult to put it together without having the picture of what it is suppose to look like in front of you. We don't have the full picture, only God does. So, when we put some of these pieces together, at best, we are only getting a small glimpse into things. The more of the pieces we fit together, the clearer the details, or image becomes, but it is a still a far cry from what the finished picture will be. We can understand prophetic events in the Bible which have already occurred, because we have the picture in front of us. History tells the story; time reveals the mystery. The future, however, remains a mystery, as time has not yet revealed its meaning. We can take the clues we have and attempt to project a possible image. This explains why there is such differing opinion when it comes to the Biblical prophecy concerning the end times. I would venture to say not one person has 100% of it correct. How can we claim to know what has not yet been revealed? God gave us clues, not the full picture; he left us 'bread crumbs' on the path to lead us in the right direction, but as yet, we are still 'in the woods'. We have to be careful in trying to understand the details that we don't forget the heart behind it all.

In writing this book, I am not attempting to give another opinion, a new revelation, or to confirm or deny any particular theory. I will state up-front, I don't have all the answers, and I don't believe anyone else does either. We would be foolish or extremely arrogant to imply we knew the mystery of God. Granted, the word of God states the mystery, or purpose of

God's plan, has been given to the church to comprehend. The most important part of this great mystery involves God's redemption of mankind through the gift of his Son. This is the essential part of the plan which man must know in order to be saved, and it is the work of the church to share this good news from God. The church has received some details of how the conclusion of his plan will play out, but they are only glimpses into the culmination of God's plan. These were given to guide the church along the way, but the final conclusion, the time line, the symbolic events and meaning, are abstract; they are shrouded in a veil of mystery. The book of Revelation states, *"But the days of the voice of the seventh angel, when he shall begin to sound, the mystery of God should be finished, as he hath declared to his servants the prophets."* *(Revelation 10:7 KJV)* The clues given to the prophets, hidden throughout the Bible, will come together and their true meaning will be revealed at that time.

In the book of Revelation it also mentions a book that is written which is in the hand of the one who sits on the throne, but it is sealed by seven seals. An angel asks, *"Who is worthy to open the book, and to loose the seals thereof?"* *(Revelation 5:2 KJV)* No man in heaven, or on the earth, or under the earth, is found worthy to open the book. The book and its contents are a mystery. Perhaps it is an outline of God's full plan, perhaps it holds the mystery of creation, of eternity, of time, but no one is found worthy; no one is able to open it. There are some things that man will never be able to answer; only God has the answers. This is exactly what happens in heaven, detailed in the book of Revelation, it says no man was found worthy, but then, a lamb comes forth from the midst of the throne, the lamb that was slain. This is Jesus! He is the only one found worthy! He is the key that opens the book, the plan of God; he IS the plan of God! God's plan will finally be fulfilled, when Jesus returns and subdues all things under his feet.

The book of Revelation is a book filled with symbols and mystery. The key we are missing is the element of time. We are finite beings, having a life cycle, a beginning and end, and as such, are one-dimensional in our way of thinking. We create time lines in order to understand our life. Unfortunately, we have tried to apply this principle to understanding the Bible. God is not a finite being like us, he is infinite. He is not subject to time, he IS time. He is without beginning or end. He is not subject to a time table or limited by a time line, he is multi-dimensional being; he is able to be in all places and in all times at once. He is all powerful, all knowing, all present, and as such, time has no hold on him. *"Holy, holy, holy, Lord God Almighty, which was, and is, and is to come." (Revelation 4:8 KJV)* This concept is difficult for us to grasp. Every child has asked the questions, "Where did God come from? Who made him?" These are questions we are not capable of answering, our minds cannot grasp the concept. Time is an element which has no significance for God.

Perhaps this may be why Israel did not understand the prophetic revelations concerning the Messiah. There were prophesies concerning a suffering messiah, (Isaiah 53; Isaiah 50:6), a messiah who would be rejected, (Isaiah 49:7; Psalm 22:6-7), a meek and gentle messiah, (Isaiah 42:2-3), as well as a messiah who would be crucified, (Psalm 22:16: Isaiah 53). There were also prophesies concerning a messiah that would be victorious, who would re-establish Israel, (Isaiah 42:13-16; Isaiah 40:1-5; Isaiah 49:7-13). In fact, there are so many prophesies describing the messiah, it seems hard for us to understand why the leaders of Israel did not recognize him. The problem was that some of these prophesies seemed to conflict, giving two separate images of the messiah. After being under Roman oppression for so long, it is understandable why the Jewish leaders wanted to give hope to the people. Undoubtedly, they must have read the scriptures of promise which held hope for the people. The people must have been very familiar with the messiah who would one day deliver them and establish Israel among the nations. The image of a messiah who would rule from Jerusalem and bring peace to the earth would have brought hope and comfort to the people during the dark times of the Roman occupation. The scriptures referring to messiah as being meek, or suffering, would have not been what the people wanted to hear. It is not uncommon even today to hear of men of God who succumb to the pressure of adapting their message in order to please the people. The religious leaders of the time must have felt pressured to preach what the people wanted to hear, in order to give them hope. This may explain why so many of them failed to recognize Jesus. Had they known his heart all along, they would have recognized him when he came.

The stark contrasts of images of the messiah in the scripture must have confused the religious leaders of the time. How were they to interpret these scriptures? Perhaps they did not realize these two different images were two different time events but the same messiah. Time was the mystery ingredient, the element which was not comprehensible. This is the same dilemma we are faced with today when we attempt to look forward into the future and try to interpret the meaning of prophesy. We don't have the understanding or the measure of time either. It has been over two thousand years since Christ promised to return, but perhaps to God it has only been two days (one day equals a thousand years). So, for us to understand when Christ will return still remains a mystery. We must not focus so much on trying to discern when it will be, but keep our focus on the fact he promised he WILL return.

Another source of mystery is in the way God has revealed things to us in the written word. We can observe in his word where he makes a statement concerning something, and then repeats the account later on, adding more detail, or a slightly different perspective. For instance, in the book of Genesis, in chapter one he tells us how he created everything in six days, and then on the seventh day he rested. In chapter two, he goes back and re-accounts the creation story. This account contains more specific details concerning how he created things, in particular, how he created man and woman, and what constituted their fall. In the gospels, there are four different viewpoints that merge into one picture of Christ. Perhaps he did things this way to help us understand the Bible is a puzzle with many pieces which come together to form a distinctive picture of God's plan for mankind. Throughout the Bible, woven into the scriptures book by book, is the image of Jesus as God's solution to the dilemma of sin and condemnation. Since the Holy Spirit is the author who dictated the Bible to his chosen servants, it is safe to assume this writing style also appears throughout the Bible, including the book of Revelation. It is a multi-dimensional book which people try to stretch out on a time line, in the attempt to put some continuity to the events described. What if those events are descriptions of things occurring simultaneously? What if they are different vantage points viewing the same time event? I am not stating that this is the case, but suggesting this as one possibility. We need to be

62

open to the Holy Spirit for understanding and not become rigid, stuck considering only one possibility. Only God has the key, the 'timing' element to these events.

This reminds me of a story I once heard of five blind men trying to describe what an elephant looked like. Each of them was touching the elephant in different areas. The first man stated an elephant was sharp and pointy, for he was feeling the elephant's tusks. The second man was feeling the elephant's trunk, so he described the elephant as long, thin and limp. The third man felt the leg and said an elephant was strong and round like a tree trunk. The fourth felt the body and stated they were all wrong; the elephant was large, flat and smooth. The last man who was touching the tail argued the elephant was nothing like how they had described it; it was thin, small and hairy at the end. While all of them were correct in their observations, not one of them had the full picture of what an elephant looked like. Perhaps this is what the book of Revelation is like, different descriptions of images that John saw regarding the end times. They are all clues, but we have to be careful how we put these clues together in order to form a picture. Having not yet seen what the end picture will look like, none of us can be certain if our theory is accurately portraying the events. Even though we may have elements correct, we may not be fitting the whole thing together properly.

What was the purpose in God's giving us these clues? He is letting us know he is in control of the future, he has the plan, and though it may not be clear to us, he knows exactly what he's doing. Perhaps it was written in this cryptic way in order to hide the true meaning and details from the enemy of our souls, the devil and his forces. Only God knows why he chose to reveal things in the way he has, thus, it is paramount for us to walk by faith, for we are not able to clearly see our way. This in itself might have been his purpose, to make us dependent upon him for the answers, thus, making us need him to find our way. If we are dependent, we will remain close to him, we will spend more time seeking him, and he will be able to keep us safely under the shadow of his wing. Isn't this what most parents do when raising their child? They give them more and more independence as they grow, while still maintaining some dependence, some rules, in order to protect their child from a world of harm that awaits them. We must not forget we have a ferocious enemy that would like nothing more than to kill, steal, and destroy us. Though we often forget the dangers out there, we forget our adversary is stalking us, 'like a roaring lion, seeking whom he may devour', he is still out there. God is defending us, keeping us safe, and not allowing the enemy to know all the details of his plans concerning us in order to safeguard us. In times of war, often the foot soldiers are not told the details of their mission. Sometimes they don't even know where they are being sent until they arrive. All of this is done in order to protect the plans of the mission from falling into enemy hands. I believe God watches over his plan in a mysterious way for many reasons, known only to him, but all of it is done out of his great love to keep us safe. He has given all he has for us, so it is not surprising to see him so protective of his children up until the end. I wonder how many have seen the mystery of Bible prophecy through this aspect, like a mother protects her young. Man wants all the answers, to know all there is to know, but having all this knowledge may not be what is in our best interest. Sometimes you just have to let go and trust God.

It is my belief the most important information for us to

concentrate on from the book of Revelation is found in the first three chapters, which is what the Spirit of God is saying to the church. He is giving us guidelines, sharing with us the secrets to overcoming, so regardless of how the events play out, the church will be ready when he comes. It is in these messages we can clearly see the heart of it all. I believe God's purpose in leading me to write this book is to point out the emphasis of God's heart and his constant plan for man throughout the ages, in order to help us keep our eyes on the prize, and not lose focus of him while we are on this journey. From beginning to end in the Bible, God repeats his desire to form us into his image and his likeness, his desire to have children to love. The messages left to the seven churches in Asia found in the book of Revelation, are a continuance of this theme. He is preparing us for his return, preparing us to be reunited with our Father. What good does it do us to know all the details of his plan, if we are not ready when he comes? In the next chapter we will deal with the words he left for his church in order to prepare them for the event of his return, in the attempt to 'glean' all we can from what he WANTS us to know. These are the areas we need to concentrate on, which include the areas we are excelling in, and the areas in which we are lacking.

These messages to the seven churches are filled with exhortations as well as strict warnings. It is a Christian's guide on how to remain faithful until he returns. There is a wealth of information in these messages. I have taken the time to study a little concerning the history of the first church, about some of the historical events unfolding around the time these messages were written, and what happened to the churches shortly thereafter. It is amazing how you can see the results of whether they heeded the advice the Spirit of God or not. Oddly enough, to this day, only one of these cities still exists under the same name, the city of Philadelphia. The city of Smyrna still exists, but has been renamed, and all of the other cities are no longer in existence. History stands as testimony of the fate of those who refuse to submit and obey God's counsel. I do not believe the historical outcome of these places is coincidental. I believe God is saying those who not only hear what the Spirit says to the church, but DO what the Spirit says, are those who will remain faithful unto the end and receive the promises he has made. He has used history, and the fate of these early places to stress a point, which is, we need to heed his warnings and obey his word. Therefore, I believe it is MOST important that we as Christians pay strict attention to what the Spirit is saying to the church through the words recorded in these first three chapters of the book of Revelation, our ability to overcome until he returns depends on our obedience to his warnings.

CHAPTER SEVEN
WHAT THE SPIRIT IS SAYING TO THE CHURCH

Jesus is going to return for us, but are we ready? What must we do to prepare ourselves for his return? The entire New Testament is filled with words, given by the Spirit of God through different vessels, written with the purpose to sanctify us and prepare us for the Lord's return. The book of Revelation was given to the disciple John by Jesus himself, through direct revelation, while he was on the island of Patmos. Jesus appeared to John in all of his glory, and then tells him to write down the things that he is about to reveal concerning the 'events hereafter'. These events have been preserved from generation to generation, and in the last generation the mystery will finally unfold.

The book of Revelation is an account of events filled with symbolism and mystery. Much debate and division has surrounded the interpretation of this book throughout the ages. In writing about the Lord's return, we will reference Revelation a great deal, but this is not an attempt to explain the book of Revelation. As previously stated, there are certain mysteries which are understood only by God himself. The attempt of this book is to present what the scripture says, not what it might mean. In looking at the book of Revelation, the most important part of the book for us to concentrate on is what is clear to understand; this is what God wants us to understand. The rest of the book, although it undoubtedly is valuable, is shrouded in mystery. The book begins with the glorious promise of Christ's return, and ends in the same manner. Jesus identifies himself in the following passage: *"I am the Alpha and Omega, the first and the last." (Rev.1:11)* He is letting us know clearly that he is at the beginning of it all, from Genesis, *"Let us make man in our image, and after our likeness"(Genesis 1:26),* to the end and fulfillment of God's plan. He alone will bring us back to the divine purpose we were created for, to be like him and spend eternity with him. He then tells John to write down his words and to send them to the seven churches which are in Asia.

The first message is for the church at Ephesus. Ephesus was a thriving metropolis, having a large population (estimated at over 200,000). It was the center of commerce in Asia in its time. Paul had spent a great deal of his time preaching in Ephesus, and a large Christian population had been established there. The church, at one point, was a strong evangelical force in the region, which established new churches throughout Asia. In this message, the Spirit acknowledges the hard work they had performed in building the kingdom; *"I know your works and your labor, and your patience". (Revelation 2:2NKJV)* He commends them for starting out so well, but then proceeds to warn them of the complacency which has crept in. *"Nevertheless, I have somewhat against you, because you have left your first love."* *(Revelation 2:4NKJV)* This message not only holds true for the church at Ephesus, but it is a warning to all Christians.

When we first come to Christ, we are passionate in our desire to serve him, but as time goes on the flame we once had in our hearts can begin to flicker. The zeal we started out with can only be compared with the euphoria of first love, when our every waking hour was consumed with thoughts of our beloved. But as time goes by, we begin to get 'comfortable' in the relationship, the passion wanes, and we can lose the 'spark' we once had. Things become a matter of routine, where our actions are carried out more from obligation or tradition then because of true passion from the heart. God never wants us to become complacent in our love for him. The message to the church at Ephesus is a wakeup call to everyone who is a believer, throughout the ages, to remember our first love for God, and to constantly work towards keeping that love vibrant. We must always remember who he is, what he has done for us, and what is his plan regarding us. We must press onwards in faith until he completes his work in us. The flame which was ignited in our hearts must always be fanned, through prayer, through praise, through devotion, so our love will deepen and grow. Isn't this the secret to any relationship? It requires time, devotion, and commitment to maintain a deepening and enduring love. If we are willing to devote our self to such an extent in an earthly, temporal relationship, how much more should we be willing to dedicate ourselves to focusing on our eternal relationship with our heavenly Father?

He does, however, commend the church in Ephesus on several points, in particular. For one thing, they avoided being deceived into following the ways of the Nicolaitanes, a sect which proclaimed to believe in Christ but were not willing to let go of the lusts and sins of this world. They tried to incorporate immorality into the church as 'acceptable' behavior. There are still those today who want it both ways. They want salvation from God, but they also want to continue in the pleasures of this world, enjoying the very sins which Christ died on the cross for. How can someone claim to love Jesus and recognize his great sacrifice for their sins, and yet continue to live in those sins? The Nicolaitanes not only participated in these beliefs, but they were in favor of teaching these principles to others as well. They were people who had no understanding of the purpose or plan of God. They wanted the salvation which Christ offered, but they did not want to submit in obedience to him as Lord. Christ did not come to set us free to sin, but to set us free from sin, and to transform us into his image.

When you really love someone, it's not hard to sacrifice what you may want to do in order to do something to make them happy instead. Those who deeply love God find it a motivation to avoid sin. Those who come to Christ out of a fear of going to Hell, eventually when that fear wears off, they return to their previous actions. If you see God as simply an authority figure rather than the love of your life, you will find it difficult to maintain your walk with him. How much easier it is when you want to please him because of your love for him, and serving him is a joy, not a sacrifice. Isn't this how we want others to feel toward us? Avoiding sin is easier when you maintain the 'first love' relationship with God as a vibrant, growing relationship.

The great promise given to the church of Ephesus is given to those who overcome such things. They will be able *"to eat from*

*the tree of life, which is in the midst of the paradise of God".
(Revelation 2:7 KJV)* This is the same tree mentioned in the beginning, in the book of Genesis, which was in the Garden of Eden! This is a promise from the Lord, he will restore us back to the state man was first created to be in, to live and walk in his presence for all eternity. Those who overcome this world and remain faithful to Christ will live forever. We will become exactly what he wants us to be, exactly what we were designed to be, eternal children of our loving Father. What a magnificent reward! God wants such good things for us. It's a shame some people think he's only interested in dictating laws and running our lives. He wants to be a part of our lives and share his love with us, helping us to have fulfilling, abundant lives.

The next message of the Spirit was to the church in Smyrna. This was a church which was suffering many things. They were composed of poor people, having very little of what the world deems as success. They were faithful to Christ even in the face of hard times and persecution. Theirs was not an easy road, but they were determined to follow Christ no matter what the cost. These Christians had their eyes on the prize, they understood God's eternal plan for them, and nothing the world had to offer could lure them away from the goal of having Christ formed in them.

The Lord praised them for their faithfulness and promised them as a reward, *"the crown of life"*, as well as eternal victory, *"He that overcomes shall not be hurt of the second death."
(Revelation 2:10-11 NKJV)* Here is a promise of God for all who follow him faithfully; they will not be in danger of condemnation. When we reach the end of this age, at the great white throne judgment, when all men shall be judged, the faithful will not be in danger of being cast out of his presence.

71

It amazes me the church in this city was not your large, successful church, as many would see things in today's way of thinking; they were not a mega-church, or a prosperous, successful church. Many have made the error of judging the success of a church on how large, or how prosperous it is. Mega churches, mega media ministries seem to draw all the attention. They seem to portray a 'look at me, this is the way to live as a victorious Christian life message. So often the small churches, the simple humble pastors, the not so affluent followers of Christ, are seen as 'moderate' successes in the world of Christianity, at best. Yet, this is where I have found the deepest faith, the greatest love and commitment.

I remember going to preach once in Juarez, Mexico. They were taking me to a small church for an evening service. We turned onto a dirt road that entered into the garbage dump of the city. I thought perhaps we were taking a shortcut. To my surprise in the midst of all this garbage, there was a city within a city. There were people, poor people, who had constructed houses out of the garbage, made of boxes, pieces of old cars, with windows made from old oven doors, and roofs made of sheets of zinc, held in place with old tires on top. There in the midst of this 'city' was one concrete block structure, it was a church. Some American Christians had come and had built a simple concrete block structure, with cement floors, for these people to have a church structure. It had an electrical cord of light bulbs which ran from outside the door into the church. I'm not sure if they were run by a generator or if there was an electrical line they were connected to. Needless to say, I was overwhelmed at the conditions. I remember saying to the Lord, "how will I preach to these people? How will I relate to them? I have no idea of what it must be like to live in this poverty."

When I entered the church, to my surprise, musicians were playing praise music, and the place was filled with people. They were not sad looking, or sitting on their make shift benches of cinder blocks and boards, they were up on their feet, dancing for the Lord! They were dressed in shabby clothes, not bathed, or with styled hair, but with big smiles on their faces. They danced around lifting their hands and praising the Lord. I was astounded! I remember in prayer saying, "Lord, don't these people know how poor they are, how desperate their circumstances are?" The Lord answered me: "Do you see these people? For many of my people, I am one among many things that they have, but to these people, I am ALL they have, and because of this, they love me with their whole heart." I remember replying to the Lord, as streams of tears ran down my face, "then Lord, you should make us all poor like them." I had never seen such pure joy, such complete love and devotion on the faces of Christians while worshiping the Lord before. I have carried that experience with me ever since. I am not promoting poverty as a way of life by telling this story. I am only trying to point out that we often measure our blessings with what we have rather than who we have.

There is such a blessing when we strip everything else away and just give ourselves totally to the Lord. Sadly, many of us in the church miss out on the blessing these people experienced. There was a 'oneness' with God they were experiencing, which I have rarely seen elsewhere. I can understand "blessed are the poor" a whole lot better since that experience.

I heard an evangelist once say over the radio, "When you get down to zero, you're walking on miracle ground." As

Christians, we need to realize it is not about how much we have, but WHO we have. This is not to say people with wealth are incapable of having a deep relationship with Christ. Our relationship with God is based on the desire of our heart, and our dedication to seeking him. What I found with these people is they had few distractions, but a great need. Unfortunately, the less need we have, or the more things we have, the more distractions we have as well, which eat up our time and energy, leaving less time for God, and less need to seek him. A deep relationship with God requires time for fellowship with him and a passion in seeking him, which applies to us all no matter what our financial status is.

The message of the Spirit to the church in Pergamum held some of the same commendations, for there were those who like in Smyrna, were facing great persecution, and they likewise were holding fast to the faith. However, there were those among them which had wavered from the truth, and had become tolerant of false teachings. Some of the false teachings contained a mixture of compromise between Christian principles and the pagan ritual practices of immorality. Pergamon was under Roman rule, and followed Roman practices by burning incense to a statue of the Roman emperor. There were those in the city who embraced Christianity, and yet they would teach it was acceptable to participate in such practices, 'acknowledging' the emperor in order not to provoke the wrath of Rome.

Human nature remains the same today; there are still some who believe it is acceptable to compromise with the world in order to keep the peace, as long as they still believe in Christ in their hearts. The Bible teaches us our actions are not irrelevant;

they say something about who we are and what we believe. The desire to "fit in" has always been a stumbling block for many in the church. How often have we seen Christians participating in worldly celebrations and events, justifying it by saying, "It doesn't mean anything? I don't believe in it, so it doesn't matter." We still find those who believe they can behave in any manner they choose, as long as they go to church on Sunday. The counsel left by the Spirit of God regarding this concept is: *"Repent, or else I will come unto thee quickly, and will fight against them with the sword of my mouth." (Revelation 2:16 KJV)* This advice remains for today's church; the word of God still declares such works to be wrong. Why risk losing God's glorious plan and purpose for your life for a few moments of indulgence in the wickedness and pleasure this world offers? Everyone knows drinking and riotous living will damage relationships, and that includes your relationship with God.

To those who overcome these things, God promises to give them *"hidden manna, and a white stone, with a new name written on it." (Revelation 2:17 KJV)* The white stone is a symbol of being found innocent before God. The hidden manna is God's deepest treasure; it is the bread of life, Jesus himself! Who would change such a treasure for a short time of 'fitting in' to this world? We, as a church, must be very careful of compromising what is right in order to fit in. This has been something the church has struggled with throughout its history, and more than often doesn't get the balance right. While we are to hate the sin, we are to love the sinner. Our mission is to love in Christ those who are lost in immorality. We tolerate their ignorance of God's word in order to show them the love of Jesus, to show them a better way, a way that requires them to repent and turn to Christ. However, we must be careful not to bend to the extreme of accepting the immoral behavior as being 'acceptable' before God.

God loved us while we were yet sinners, and we need to follow his example toward others, remembering we are here to bring change to their lives by bringing them the love of God and the plan of salvation from sin. I have seen both extremes, those who say God is love, so therefore anything goes in the church, who tolerate all lifestyles, so as not to be judgmental, as well as those who use the word of God as a weapon to judge and condemn anyone who is less than perfect. We can only find the right balance by following the example of Jesus. He did not judge and condemn sinners, he told them to go and sin no more. He showed love, while teaching people the ways of God, encouraging them to repent and return to their Father, who would forgive them. His example is the model the church should apply as to how to walk in this world, in order to reach a lost world with the love of God, while being careful to avoid the danger of 'fitting in' to the sinful ways of the world.

The letter of the Spirit to the church in Thyatira was to a church in compromise as well. There were those who had worked hard and were compassionate, obedient followers of Christ, but there were also those who were not so faithful. The city was a merchant city which had a great following of people who worshiped the goddess Diana. In this religion, women were the leaders who were in charge of the religious services, which often included immoral participation from its converts. As many of these pagan followers were converted to Christ, some wanted to continue to hold on to certain practices they had enjoyed in their former religion. Women who were used to being in charge found it difficult to fit in to their new found faith. While the promise of forgiveness of sin and eternal life was appealing, they still wanted to hold on to a position of prominence in the new Christian church. They were used to being in control, of thinking of themselves as the spiritual leaders, and a humble, submissive spirit was a foreign concept to them. They also wanted to continue to incorporate the immoral practices they were accustomed to. Christianity is not to be political; we are not to strive for a place of honor or prominence. We are all his children, and as such, there should not be a power struggle for control in his church. We are all to submit to his leadership, and be led by his Spirit into the unity of the faith. We are meant to think of others first and to serve one another in brotherly love. This concept was new to many of the converts in Thyatira, and while many embraced it willingly, there were those who were not so eager to let go of their status or control.

The church has continued to struggle with these issues throughout the ages. The desire for control, for power over others, is found in the very nature of man. Our history, and the many wars this nature has spawned, is a testament to this. The devil has always used this hidden desire in man against him. He has tempted mankind throughout the ages, and he tempted Jesus in the same matter. He took Jesus to a high mountain top and showed him all the kingdoms of the earth; then he offered him all of them, if he, (Jesus), would just bow down and worship him. The Lord's reply is the answer for all who are tempted in the same manner, *"Get thee hence, Satan; for it is written, thou shalt worship the Lord thy God, and him only shalt thou serve." (Matthew 4:10 KJV)* God alone is supreme. He alone is worthy to be worshiped. He is in control, and we should carry out his will and not our own. The desire to put oneself on a pedestal and to have dominion and control over others is evil. This is what caused the fall of Satan, and it will surely bring destruction to anyone who gives in to these evil temptations. There is no room in God's church for this nature. There is only one Lord. A body cannot function correctly with more than one head. While God does put people in positions of leadership within the church body, there is only one head, Jesus himself.

There was a great struggle going on in the church in Thyatira and God promised those who held such immoral practices would be cast into great tribulation unless they repented. In his admonition to the church in Thyatira, the Lord remembered the faithful and acknowledged them by letting them know since they have faithfully endured this great struggle, he would not put any other burden on them. He told them to hold fast to what they already had until he comes. The Lord is told them and to us today, to hold on to the faith, to keep up the good work until he comes. The reward of the faithful is to rule over the nations with him. He is willing to share his power with us, as long as we remember he is the head. It is also stated that we will be given 'the morning star'. This is another name, or symbol, for Jesus. We will be given Jesus; to be with him, and rule with him for all eternity. The danger of seeking power and control can be overcome by seeking the Lord to give us a 'servant heart', as he had. The Bible says he did not come to be served, but to serve, and to give his life as a ransom for man. He also said if we want to be great in his kingdom, we need to become the servant of all. This is the heart God wants us to have, a heart which is content to serve God, to serve others, and not a heart which is looking for personal gain or accolade.

The harshest rebuke is for the church at Sardis. The Spirit states this church bears the name of Christianity, but in actuality is a dead church. Granted, this was not true of all of the believers in Sardis, but a vast group in the church was just 'playing' church. The little good they were doing was in danger of dying as well. He tells them to strengthen the little good which remained. He counsels them to repent, to remember the message they first received, and to return to the truth. He warns them he will return as a thief in the night, when they least expect it, and they will be found not watching or waiting for his return. In other words, they will be left behind! What a message for the church of today! This is a warning from the Lord to those who still 'play' church. They go to church on Sunday, listen to the message, nodding their heads, but they never take it to heart. They don't apply the word to their lives. They simply fulfill their duty in going, and then live the rest of the week as they see fit. There is no fountain of life in them, no compassion springing up. They have no desire to spread the good news, or to share Christ with anyone else. Their faith is not an important aspect of their life; it is just a tradition, a ritual that is carried out to appease God, in the event there is an afterlife. God refers to such believers, and such religious establishments as 'dead' churches. Why? They have never surrendered their lives or their hearts to Christ. They have not been born again into the Kingdom of God. The church is meant to be the living, breathing, loving arm of the Lord, extended to the needs of humanity. It is to be the reflection of him, carrying out the mission of redemption and reconciliation to all. It is our school, the training ground, for preparing us to be with him for eternity. Thank God, however, even in the midst of 'dead' churches, there are always a few who follow after the truth, who truly love God.

In Sardis, there were those few who had not defiled themselves; God's promise to them, and to all who are in a dead church, was they would be clothed in white garments and their names would remain in the book of life. God would not blot out their names; he would confess them before the Father! This indicates to us those who say they are Christian's, who say they believe in Christ, yet never really give themselves to him, are fooling themselves into believing they will end up in heaven. Christianity is more than a set of beliefs; it is a way of life. Just because someone believes there is a God, doesn't mean they love God or follow in his way. The Bible says the devil and his demons 'believe' in God, but they don't follow him. True belief requires more, it requires obedience. God wants us to love him, to be devoted to him, to desire to be with him as much as he desires to be with us. True faith is a living relationship, not a dead religious tradition. As state in John chapter three, "we must be born again". We need to come to Christ, surrendering our lives to him in order to be 'adopted' into the family of God and have our names written in the Book of Life.

We make the choice to believe in him and to become reconciled to our Heavenly Father. His desire is that none should perish, and that all would come to the knowledge of the truth, but the choice is up to us. We choose if we are going to give him first place in our lives, if we are going to serve him or not. A so called 'dead' Christian is one who may intellectually believe in the existence of Christ, but has never made a personal commitment to him. They follow a set of religious beliefs without having a personal relationship with Christ.

The church in Philadelphia was perhaps the most commended of the seven churches. What made the believers in

Philadelphia so different? It says they had just a little strength, but what little they had they used to the fullest. They held on fast to Christ, using every ounce of strength they had, in other words, with their whole heart. They were faithful to his teachings, not just hearers of his word, but doers of his word. God promised to keep them from the hour of temptation which would come upon the earth. This is an eternal promise to all who are faithful and cling to him with their whole heart. God will spare such believers from the great judgment which will come upon the earth. Their reward is to be a pillar in the temple of God, to have the name of God and of God's city, the New Jerusalem, written on them. They will be a part of the city's foundation, a pillar in the city.

The message to the church in Philadelphia speaks prophetically to the end of this age. It is a promise that the faithful will be spared; it is a promise to be part of the New Jerusalem, that beautiful heavenly city. It is amazing to see the believers who were described as only having a little strength receive such a wonderful reward. It gives us all hope. We don't have to be giants of faith, we simply have to believe with our whole heart, and trust in his word, which tell us: *"we can do all things through Christ which strengthens us."* *(Philippians 4:13)* What great reward awaits those who truly love the Lord! God uses this message to the church in Philadelphia to encourage and inspire us, to let us know it is worth the effort, all the hard work, all the dying to our own lusts and worldly desires. There is a great promise of reward to those who are faithful. The city of Philadelphia exists to this day, standing as a historical testament to God's promise to those who overcome the world and remain faithfully devoted to him. God wants us to know whatever the sacrifice, whatever the price we pay; it will be worth it all!

Finally, to the church in Laodicia, the Spirit of God sends yet another warning. This church is described as a 'lukewarm' church. God tells them he wished they were either hot or cold, but because they were lukewarm, he will spit them out of his mouth. What made him make such a strong statement? What was their weakness? They thought they were rich, having everything and in need of nothing. In other words, they were a self-sufficient church. They were comfortable with things as they were, and had no need to seek God for anything else. They were a prideful church, which felt it had 'arrived', and they had no need for further improvement. This is a very dangerous attitude for a church to have. Can you imagine a mere mortal man thinking he has no need of God? We may not make such a statement in words, but our actions and our lifestyle often speaks volumes. What man can add more time to his life? Who is able to stop the moment of death from happening? Who can save a sick or dying child? Who can stand the power of a hurricane, or survive a flood? With all our technology and abilities, we are still helpless in front of some of life's greatest challenges. When we think we have no need of anything more from God, we become independent from him. We are trusting in our own abilities and not in God; in essence, we are telling God, 'I don't need you". If we think we are able to make it on our own, God will let us attempt to do just that. God does not force himself on us; neither does he make us do his will. It is our choice to make, a right which he gave us, and he respects our right to choose, even when we make the most catastrophic choices. Our own pride, to do things ourselves and not seek his help, becomes our downfall, for no man can make it without God. Whether we realize it or not, this attitude is nothing more than rebellion. We have made a choice to do our own thing, to be our own 'god'. What arrogance to think we know more than God does about what is best for us! We may not think these thoughts, or look at things in this light, but our actions often display this attitude.

God tells the church in Laodicia even though they felt they were rich, and not lacking in anything, in truth, they were naked, poor, and miserable. He counseled them to buy some of the medicinal eye salve their city was so famous for producing, and use it themselves, because they were blinded by their own pride. Although his rebuke is harsh, he reminds them it is because he loves them saying: *"as many as I love, I rebuke and chasten."* *(Revelation 3:19 KJV)* He gives a wonderful promise here; *"Behold, I stand at the door and knock: if any man hears my voice, and opens the door, I will come in to him, and will sup with him, and he with me."* *(Revelation 3:20 KJV)* What a statement of hope to end the messages of the Spirit to these seven churches! He promises to knock on the heart of all men, waiting on them to open the door and invite him in. Everyone is invited to open the door, and if they do, he promises he will come in and have fellowship with them. This is God's invitation to all, revealing his great love for mankind. Imagine who he is, and all he has already done for us, and then for him to make the statement HE stands at the door and knocks. We should be on our faces seeking his forgiveness for rejecting his great love and mercy, looking to find our way back to him, and yet he came to look for us, he stands at the door of our hearts, patiently knocking, waiting for us to open the door! How can people doubt God's existence, or his love for us? Who else would have the patience to endure all we have done, all of our arrogant, neglectful, selfish attitudes, and still, as a loving Father, be willing to forgive us? His love and grace, his mercy and patience, are immeasurable.

He ends his message to the church of Laodicea by saying, whoever overcomes will get to sit on his throne with him. We will get to sit in his lap! What a beautiful description to remind us he is our loving Father. While his greatness may cause us to tremble, still the depths of his love invite us to come, as little children, to sit in his lap! Why would he care so much for someone so small? If we go back to the beginning, we can see all along how his purpose and his love for his children has not changed. He wants to re-establish the fellowship he created man to have with him, to walk and talk one on one in the garden with us, as he did with Adam and Eve before the fall.

I could not write this book about the coming of his kingdom, without including the messages given by the Holy Spirit to these churches. This is his revelation as to the purpose and promise of his kingdom. It is the unveiling of his eternal plan. It contains the secrets of overcoming for all of us who wish to be a part of his kingdom. We must not be fearful of what lies ahead. In all things we must commit ourselves to him, in order to avoid the ways of the world, the lust of the flesh, the pride of human nature, the deception of riches and conceit, and faithfully follow him. We must maintain a loving obedience, even in the face of trials and temptations, trusting in his word and his faithfulness, regardless of the situations we face. We must trust in his strength, and the guidance of his Spirit to overcome all these things, and hold fast to the faith, so we will be found faithful when he returns.

CHAPTER EIGHT

"Henceforth there is laid up of me a crown of righteousness, which the Lord, the righteous judge, shall give me at that day; and not to me only, but unto all them also that love his appearing." (II Timothy 4:8)

We have a promise from the Lord that he will one day return, and while this is widely accepted among Christians, are we waiting for him, are we loving his appearing? The scripture above tells us God has prepared a reward for all of us who have served him faithfully, all of those who "love his appearing". What does this mean? I have spoken to Christians concerning the return of the Lord on numerous occasions. I have spoken to people of different age groups, different nationalities, and those living throughout the country. While most realize the Lord may return at any time, the majority do not seem to be in any hurry for the Lord to return. I have heard statements such as, "I want the Lord to return, but first, I'd like to get married and have children", or "I still have a lot I would like to do before the Lord returns." This doesn't sound like comments of people who are anxious for his return or that "loves his appearing".

Let me say here that not everyone holds this opinion. Not everyone who loves the Lord is hesitant about his return. I think the measure of our desire to see him pretty much indicates the level of love we have in our heart for him. Some may not agree, but if you really love someone with your whole heart and you're separated from seeing them, what's the one thing you want more than anything, to be reunited with them, right? Can you imagine how the heart of God feels? Here he is waiting for the day to finally bring all his children home, planning every detail for this great reunion, and some don't seem that concerned or desirous for the event to occur? What's wrong with this picture? I believe we, the church, need to seriously examine our hearts concerning our attitude. How would any bridegroom feel if upon asking his intended to marry him her response was, "well maybe someday, but I'm in no hurry to be with you: I've got other things more important to do at the moment"? Or perhaps, "let me check out my options and I'll get back to you"? In essence, isn't this the attitude many are displaying?

Most people associate the coming of the Lord with the end of the world. The prevailing attitude seems to be, when the Lord returns it will be the end of life, the end of the world, even among Christians. It's no wonder people do not appear to be desirous of the Lord's return. As long as they see it as an "end" instead of as a "beginning", we are not going to see people anxiously waiting for the Lord to appear. Although the reason for this perception may vary, it is based in part on a lack of understanding of what the word of God says regarding his return and the establishment of his kingdom. In order to understand it clearly, we have to keep in mind what God's purpose was for creating mankind to begin with. The main purpose of this book has been to bring about an understanding of God's eternal plan for us, so we might work toward the fulfillment of his plan. Many in the church have equated "being

86

with the Lord" as being "dead", and understandably, no one looks forward to death. The scripture tells us death is an enemy which Jesus has conquered, and he will one day destroy in the lake of fire. God did not create us to "die"; our choice to sin brought about a death sentence. God's gift to us is life. He wants us to live! In truth, up until this point in time, in order to go be with the Lord, it has involved dying, or leaving this earthly body, but death will end when he returns. The Bible states when the Lord returns for his church, those who are alive at his coming will be "caught up" to meet him in the air. *"For this we say unto you by the word of the Lord, that we which are alive and remain unto the coming of the Lord shall not prevent them which are asleep. For the Lord himself shall descend from heaven with a shout, with the voice of the archangel, and with the trump of God: and the dead in Christ shall rise first: Then we which are alive and remain shall be caught up together with them in the clouds, to meet the Lord in the air: and so shall we ever be with the Lord." (I Thessalonians 4: 15-17 KJV)* The generation alive at his return will not have to die in order to join the Lord!

Another point concerning the will and purpose of God is in understanding his desire to reconcile man to God and establish his kingdom within us. While we think of death as being the time of being reunited with God, or entering the kingdom of heaven, which it is, the kingdom of God is not just in heaven. The Kingdom of God is wherever the King is. When we receive Jesus into our heart, he becomes one with us, establishing his kingdom within us. Jesus established his kingdom by his sacrifice on the cross, by paying the price for redeeming us. When we receive him in our hearts, he enters and establishes his kingdom in us. But the Bible also speaks of his return to receive us. We walk in the spiritual realm in his kingdom now, and when our spirit leaves our body, our spirit is taken to heaven to be with him. When he returns, we will be reunited with him without having to leave our body, without having to die; our bodies will be transformed, and those who have died will have their bodies resurrected.

In addressing the concept of "it all coming to an end", the Word of God clearly teaches life is not over for the believer, it is just the beginning. *"Behold, I shew you a mystery; we shall not all sleep, but we shall all be changed, in a moment, in the twinkling of an eye, at the last trump: for the trumpet shall sound, and the dead shall be raised incorruptible, and we shall be changed. For this corruptible must put on incorruption, and this mortal must put on immortality."* (*I Corinthians 15: 51-53 KJV*) Those alive at his return will NEVER have to die; they will have their bodies changed from a deteriorating state, to an eternal state, no more aging, no more pains and problems! We will not be separated from our love ones ever again! Best of all, we will see Jesus and be with him forevermore! This is definitely something to be excited about, and to look forward to! Why do we think it will be an end to our dreams and our goals? Didn't God give us those goals and aspirations? There will still be work for us to do. We will be with our loved ones; we will continue working for the good of God's kingdom. The thing which will come to an end is the evil man causes to his fellow man. Can you imagine a world where there is no evil in it, where there is no fear of dying or of disease? We will finally have the chance to LIVE! We will be able to succeed without all the pitfalls, without the constant attacks of the enemy. We won't just be sitting up in heaven playing on harps. We will be eternal beings, with an eternity to learn about our Father, his design and plan for us, and all he has created. The word of God also indicates, in the book of Revelation, we will rule and reign with him. In other words, he will have jobs and responsibilities for us to carry out; life, a much better existence, will continue. God originally designed us to subdue the earth, to rule over and care for all the creatures on this planet. He designed us to have fellowship with him, to be in daily communion with him. His plan is to "raise" us to be like him. We are finally going to be back to where we were meant to be all along.

When we take a look at the plan of God, the sequence of events is as follows:

God creates man in his image and his likeness;
Man disobeys God, and his sin brings about his death;
God sends his laws for man to follow;
Man continues to fail to obey God;
God sends his son Jesus to pay for the sentence of sin over man;
Jesus dies on the cross, shedding his blood for our atonement.
He is raised from the dead and victoriously establishes his kingdom in the believer.
The Holy Spirit empowers the church to spread the good news of God's redemption plan;
Jesus returns for his church, catching them up to meet him in the air;
Jesus defeats Satan and throws him into the lake of fire along with all evil and death;
God spends eternity enjoying his children, forming them into his likeness.

This is rather simplified, but it gives us an idea of God's plan for mankind; granted, these events are separated by time, but it presents an over-all picture of his plan, one which he had from the beginning of creation. Basically, God had a plan, man took a detour, then God provided the solution, resulting in "His kingdom come, His will be done, on earth as it is in Heaven."

I would love to finally be able to succeed in serving God without the constant attacks from the enemy, without sickness and fatigue wearing me down. I would love to see my children flourish in the love of the Lord, without seeing all the struggles and trials, all the frustrations and heartaches. We, as the people of God, will finally be able to walk in freedom, and live without all the stumbling blocks and obstacles the enemy puts in our path to hinder us. While we, who have accepted Christ, are on the path in this life, we are in a constant battle with forces of the enemy which bombard us continually, and our fleshly nature continues to war against our spirit as well. But who wouldn't want to see the end to these struggles, or the defeat of Satan?

This doesn't mean we won't have anything to do. There will still be work to do, things to learn, goals and achievements to reach. What we won't have is an enemy tempting us at every turn. We will not have the battle of our carnal flesh, the lusts which drive us to such disastrous consequences. We will have glorified bodies, which are not limited in ability, or subject to weakness or disease. We will not be like robots; we will still have our own personalities and uniqueness. We will have knowledge and memory; we will know each other, *"For now we see through a glass, darkly; but then face to face; now I know in part; but then shall I know even as also I am known."* (*I Corinthians 13:12 KJV*) We will be with our loved ones, our family and friends, who are also a part of God's church. Loving relationships were a design God created, so why would they disappear? In other words, the good things God created will remain. The evil ways of the world will end. It may sound like paradise, but that's actually how God created man to live, in harmony with him and with those around him. We will finally get the opportunity to live how he created us to live. The best part of all is we will see him! We will be able to ask him all the things we have wanted to ask. We will be able to receive his wisdom and guidance for every need or question we might have. We won't be all alone, (which we aren't now if we walk in the Spirit), but then he will walk with us, not just in spirit, but in a real, tangible way. The night before Jesus was crucified, he prayed this prayer to the Father: *"Father, I want those you have given me to be with me where I am, and to see my glory, the glory you have given me because you have loved me before the creation of the world."* *(John 17:24 NIV)* His desire is for us to be with him forever! His return will be the biggest family reunion ever!

I love to imagine what it will be like. I will see my family, those who have gone on to be with the Lord, and they will have so much to show me of the wonders they have learned by having been in the presence of the Lord. I will get to meet my Christian family from all over the world, and not only of this age, but those who lived before me. Can you imagine meeting Mary and asking her how it felt to hold the Lord of Glory in her arms? Or perhaps to talk with Peter about seeing the miracle of all those fish filling his boat. What about hearing King David tell the story of how he brought down Goliath? I would like to ask Noah how he managed to take care of all those animals on a moving ship. What about hearing Moses describe the experience of walking through the Red Sea, or Paul telling of his many journeys? One of the most amazing experiences (when you are in a strange place and don't know anyone) happens when you meet someone who is also a Christian and begin to share your joint faith in Christ. Before long, you have a new friend, and you feel an amazing love and oneness with this person. You go away from the encounter exhilarated, blessed beyond words. Just imagine the experience multiplied by a thousand and more! It is most certainly a family reunion I don't want to miss!

It amazes me there are Christians who aren't in a hurry for this to happen. Why wouldn't you be? Here again, we have to wonder why there are those who say they love the Lord, but don't seem to be desirous of his return. Perhaps they don't fully understand what the scripture says concerning his return. The generation which is alive at his return will escape the most traumatic event all humans have had to endure; they won't have to face death. I don't want to die, and I don't think anyone else does either. It isn't because I fear what will happen after death, for I have God's promise, *"While we are at home in the body, we are absent from the Lord; but we are confident, I say, and willing rather to be absent from the body and to be present with the Lord."* *(II Corinthians 5:6;8 KJV)* The Lord has promised eternal life to all those who believe and follow him. I can't imagine what those who don't know him must suffer. How do you face your own mortality or the death of a loved one, when you have no assurance, no idea of whether you will continue to exist, or ever see your loved ones again? For those who don't know the Lord, death must be the most frightening thing there can be. But for those of us who have come to the knowledge of Christ, we have a peace, a confidence, death is not the end.

Years ago, a dear Christian brother informed us that his beloved mother had passed away. She was a wonderful Christian lady who lived well into her eighties. My husband was able to attend her funeral and told me it was such a blessing. All of her loved ones were rejoicing because she was finally at home with her beloved savior. It was like a great family reunion with everyone hugging each other, singing songs of praise to the Lord, and sharing wonderful stories of the life of this dear mother. But at this funeral home there was another funeral being held as well. This funeral was for a young man who had passed away. This family was not in the Lord. My husband told me the cries and wails coming out of the other room were heart wrenching. There was such desperation, such hopelessness and pain. What a difference knowing Jesus makes.

Still, understandably, the experience of 'dying' is an uncomfortable thought. I have stated on occasion, and have heard others say as well, "I am not afraid of death, just the experience of dying." How will it feel? How will it happen? Will we suffer; will we struggle? What will happen to our loved ones? All of these questions are what makes the subject of death such a difficult one. When Christ returns, we will be caught up with him, and we won't have to die to go to be with him! We will be spared the anguish of this separation experience. Our loved ones in Christ will be caught up with us! And then life, real victorious, abundant, full of joy, eternal life, will begin! I can't imagine why anyone would say they want Jesus to come back someday, but not right now. What in this world is more significant, or what do we need yet to accomplish which is greater or more important than his return? It certainly can't be because we don't want to miss out on the 'death experience'. When the Lord returns, we will be able to succeed in being all we have ever hoped or dreamed about. We will not experience failure or death. I believe if the church would embrace the truth about his return and what it means, we would hear more Christians talking and praying about his return. We would see a lot more excitement and preparation for his return among believers. We would "love his appearing."

Oh, how he longs to see our faces as we look upon him in all his glory and beauty! How long he has waited for that moment. He is ever close to us, but we don't react as if he was. We often are so busy we ignore him. It will be impossible to ignore him when he is right before our eyes. All the foolish priorities and waste of our time will melt away from our thoughts. We will see him as he is, and we will finally be able to comprehend his worth! The great treasure of his love will be evident, and we will realize he was all we needed from the very start. His heart will be filled with joy that will flow out and envelope us like loving arms, and we will finally know him, his love and his peace, the depths of which we can only imagine.

While the return of the Lord is a great and glorious homecoming event for those who believe in Christ, it is a fearful, horrendous thing for those who have rejected him. While we will be rejoicing in the greatest family reunion of all times, those who have not chosen to follow Christ will be experiencing a very different thing. The Bible refers to life on the earth during this time period as a great time of tribulation. Why would anyone choose to stay behind and live through such an experience? Since we do not know the day or hour when the Lord will return, it is important we make things right with God on a day to day, moment to moment basis. Why would people put off accepting the loving savior, Jesus Christ, and miss out on all the wonderful things he has for them. Why do they run the risk of not being able to go with him when he returns? They just don't understand what is at stake, or what awaits them if they continue to ignore God's knocking on their door. The church HAS to do all it can, we have to do a better job at presenting Jesus to the world if we want to see them accept God's offer and be saved from the terrible fate which awaits those who turn their backs on God. The Bible concludes with the attitude the church should have concerning his return: *"Surely I come quickly. Amen. Even so, come, Lord Jesus." (Revelation 22:20)*

CHAPTER NINE
THE RETURN OF THE LORD

The word of God has a great deal to say concerning future events; many of the details, like puzzle pieces, are hidden throughout the Bible. Some of their meaning is fairly clear, while other passages are a mystery. Some scriptures seem to be very similar, even though they may have been written centuries apart. Certain events seem to be referenced repeatedly, but the order in which these events occur is often a subject of much debate. Without God giving us the revelation of how these events piece together, the best we can do is speculate. I am going to list some of the prophetic scriptures and attempt to categorize them for the purpose of examination, in an attempt to 'piece' some of the puzzle pieces together. This is not an attempt to interpret their meaning, but to familiarize us with the 'clues'. This may help us to recognize the picture as God orchestrates it into his final masterpiece. Knowing the signs given to us in the word of God will help us to prepare so we will not be caught by surprise as these prophetic events begin to unfold on earth.

Here is some of the scriptural proof which refers to the return of the Lord:

"But Christ has indeed been raised from the dead, the first fruits of those who have fallen asleep; for since death came through a man, the resurrection of the dead comes also through a man. For as in Adam all die, so in Christ will all be made alive. But each in his own turn: Christ the first fruits; then, when he comes, those who belong to him. Then the end will come, when he hands over the kingdom to God the Father after he has destroyed all dominion, authority and power; for he must reign until he has put all his enemies under his feet. The last enemy to be destroyed is death." I (Corinthians 15:20-26 NIV)

"Behold, I shew you a mystery; we shall not all sleep, but we shall all be changed, in a moment, in the twinkling of an eye, at the last trump: for the trumpet shall sound, and the dead shall be raised incorruptible, and we shall be changed. For this corruptible must put on incorruption, and this mortal must put on immortality." (I Corinthians 15: 51-53 KJV)

"For this we say unto you by the word of the Lord, that we which are alive and remain unto the coming of the Lord shall not prevent them which are asleep. For the Lord himself shall descend from heaven with a shout, with the voice of the archangel, and with the trump of God: and the dead in Christ shall rise first: Then we which are alive and remain shall be caught up together with them in the clouds, to meet the Lord in the air: and so shall we ever be with the Lord." (I Thessalonians 4:15-17 KJV)

CHARLENE RAMIREZ

Jesus said, *"No one knows about that day or hour, not even the angels in heaven, nor the Son, but only the Father. As it was in the days of Noah, so it will be at the coming of the Son of Man. For in the days before the flood, people were eating and drinking, marrying and giving in marriage, up to the day Noah entered the ark; and they knew nothing about what would happen until the flood came and took them all away. That is how it will be at the coming of the Son of Man. Two men will be in the field; one will be taken, and the other left. Two women will be grinding with a hand mill; one will be taken and the other left. Therefore keep watch, because you do not know on what day your Lord will come."* (Matthew 24:36-42 NIV)

"Verily I say unto you, that this generation shall not pass, till all these things be done. Heaven and earth shall pass away, but my words shall not pass away. But of that day and that hour knoweth no man, no not the angels which are in heaven, neither the Son, but the Father. Take ye heed, watch and pray; for ye know not when the time is." (Mark 13: 30-33 KJV)

"Be careful, or your hearts will be weighed down with dissipation, drunkenness and the anxieties of life, and that day will close on you unexpectedly like a trap, for it will come upon all those who live on the face of the whole earth. Be always on the watch, and pray that you may be able to escape all that is about to happen, and that you may be able to stand before the Son of Man" (Luke 21:34-36NIV)

These scriptures found in different parts of the Bible, reference the event most commonly referred to as the 'rapture', (although this word is not used in the scripture, but it is the commonly accepted term for "being caught up"). There are those who believe this event will not take place, stating it is far-fetched to believe people will literally disappear all over the earth. The word of God indicates the contrary. There are some who say the term 'caught up' refers to being separated or hidden apart, and does not mean to literally be taken up in the clouds. The word of God says concerning this event, we will be caught up in the air. We do not have to understand how it will take place or the science of it all, in order to believe it. Is there anything impossible for God? This is an issue of faith; either God said what he meant, and is able to accomplish it, or not. We do not know how God made the DNA of each living thing to contain a full blueprint as to his unique makeup, but we can acknowledge it exists whether we understand all of its dynamics or not. In the same way, we can choose to accept God will literally change the cells in our body from a deteriorating mortal state into a eternal immortal state in an instant, and he will then have these immortal bodies, who are not subject to the laws of gravity any longer, 'fly up' in the air to meet with him. We may not be able to explain how this can scientifically happen any more than we can explain the complexities of DNA or the dimensions of the universe, but we can choose to accept with God all things are possible. There are those who believe the scripture is speaking figuratively and not to be taken literally, again, I am presenting what the Word of God states. Because we don't understand it doesn't mean it isn't possible. The plan, the purpose, and the answer, all of these things were accomplished in Jesus. He is the good news! He is the King, the heart of the Kingdom!

The church cannot lose sight of its mission. These are critical times, critical hours, as this dispensation of time draws to an end. If we look at the signs of the times, the fulfillment of prophecy given through the word of God, one can't help but see man's time is reaching its conclusion, and God's plan is reaching its fulfillment. Jesus gave us some clear hints as to the end of this age: *"Ye shall hear of wars and rumors of wars: see that ye be not troubled: for all these things must come to pass, but the end is not yet. For nation shall rise against nation, and kingdom against kingdom: and there shall be famines, and pestilences, and earthquakes, in divers places." (Matthew 24:7 KJV)* What generation before has seen such great wars as those seen over the last hundred years? What about the great famines where thousands of lives have been lost in Africa alone, or the increase of earthquakes all over the earth? But the greatest sign to me is in this verse: *"And this gospel of the kingdom shall be preached in all the world for a witness unto all nations: and then shall the end come." (Matthew 24:14 KJV)* Never, in the history of man, has the ability existed to reach the entire world with the message of Jesus Christ. Through the media, by satellite, the gospel is literally being preached around the globe. This is but one sign which indicates the end of this age is drawing near. Another distinct sign is Israel becoming a nation again, which also happened in this generation. Thus, sign upon sign continue to mount, pointing to the conclusion that the return of Jesus Christ is quickly approaching.

This is the time for the church to have faith! It is time for us to lift up our heads and rejoice, for the redemption of God draws near. But what of the statement Jesus made, *"Will he find faith when he returns?" (Luke 18:8)* His words, although a cause for concern also contains a precious promise, he is returning! He spoke of a kingdom, the kingdom of his Father, when he taught us to pray, *"Thy kingdom come, thy will be done, on earth as it is in heaven." (Matthew6:10 KJV)* It is

God's will that we pray for his kingdom to come and his will to be done on EARTH as it is in heaven. He desires his kingdom be established on earth in us now, for the King of the kingdom inhabits our hearts and lives, and lives and moves through us; but the word of God also tells us very clearly, Jesus, our King, will one day return for us. In the book of Acts, after the resurrection of Christ, it states that many saw him during a forty day period. He told them many things concerning the kingdom of God, and then in an amazing moment, they watched as he was taken up into the clouds. While they were standing there in awe gazing up, two angels appeared and told them: *"Men of Galilee,"* they said, *"why do you stand here looking into the sky? This same Jesus, who has been taken from you into heaven, will come back in the same way you have seen him go into heaven."* *(Acts 1:11 NIV)* They were proclaiming that Christ would one day return! This is confirmed throughout the teachings of Jesus, where he stated numerous times about the return of the 'son of man'. In the letter to the Thessalonians, Paul states: *"For the Lord himself shall descend from heaven with a shout, with the voice of the archangel, and with the trump of God; and the dead in Christ shall rise first: then we which are alive and remain shall be caught up together with them in the clouds, to meet the Lord in the air; and so shall we ever be with the Lord."* *(I Thessalonians 4:16-17 KJV)* The church refers to this promised event as the Rapture. It is going to be the greatest reunion of all time.

There are those who discount we will literally be caught up in the air, and I am not attempting to explain how or when this will occur, I am simply presenting what the scripture says regarding this event. Why do we find it so hard to believe, and therefore conclude this obviously must mean something else?

We are dealing with God, the same God who had the power to create all of this; would it be impossible for him to do? There are many things in the word of God that require a leap of faith. Jesus said he is going to return for us, and I believe him. God has put so much into his plan from beginning to end with the utmost care and detail; his design is flawless. His purpose is to be united with his people and restore the relationship he created us to have with him from the beginning, and he fulfilled his promise by sending his Son to complete his plan. I find it hard to believe he would not continue to follow his own plan and complete the promises he has made, not after he has poured all of himself into the success of the plan. Jesus will return and the will of God will be fulfilled on earth as it is in heaven, just as he has promised in his word. Not a detail written in his word will go unfulfilled. The scripture promises heaven and earth will pass away but his word will never pass away. It will all happen exactly as he said it would.

There is also much debate around this event in regards to when it will take place. There are some who believe this will happen before the period known as the great tribulation will occur. They reference the scripture where John is 'taken up' into the Spirit in the beginning of chapter four in the book of Revelation as a clue the church will likewise be 'taken up' before the events of the rest of the book play out. Those who believe this scenario are referred to as pre-tribulation believers. They refer to the message to the church in Philadelphia, where the Lord promised the faithful will be spared the hour of temptation which God will pour out on the earth; they also reference these other scriptures: *"Much more then, being now justified by his blood, we shall be saved from wrath through him." (Romans 5:9 KJV); "And to wait for his Son from heaven; whom he raised from the dead, even Jesus, which delivered us from the wrath to come." (I Thessalonians 1:10 KJV)* and finally, *"For God hath not appointed us to wrath, but to obtain salvation by our Lord Jesus Christ." (I Thessalonians 5:9 KJV)* These scriptures make it clear God will pour his anger out on all those rebellious people who chose to reject his many efforts to reach them, and hatefully turned away from his loving attempts to save them. They chose wickedness and evil over the love and mercy of God. They hated the things of God; they hated his children, and delighted in causing suffering to their fellow man. The punishment they will receive is God's justice, his sentence carried out for their continual rejection of him and all which is good. In no way will God take pleasure or enjoy carrying out this sentence. His will is that none should perish, but that all would come to knowledge of his plan of forgiveness through Jesus Christ.

The consequences of rejecting God's love, his way, have been clearly stated, giving all a chance to reconsider and choose wisely. He will not force anyone to choose him. It must be of our own free will we choose him. Those who have followed him faithfully will not be subject to his wrath or judgment which is reserved at the end for those who refuse to follow him. He will not punish us for being obedient. No parent deliberately and unjustly punishes the child who has obeyed. We can be certain whenever the rapture does occur, regardless of what may happen on the earth, God will spare us in his loving hand. He knows the difference between his children who serve him, and those who serve evil. God is able to "take us out" or cover us in his hand through it all. Their theory has some merit, but the danger is in thinking that we will be spared from any kind of suffering or tribulation. If we believe this theory, we may be tempted to not prepare to endure to the end. Again, in returning to the messages to the churches in Revelation, we see that these churches had to endure and to "overcome" until the end. To paint a picture which promises no suffering is not realistic or Biblical. We all hope he comes sooner rather than later, but history teaches us that there have been many Christians who have suffered for their faith. Why do we believe we will be excluded? We all hope so, but since no one knows the day or the hour, isn't it wiser to be prepared, to be strong in faith, able to endure persecution, if necessary, for the cause of Christ, and remain faithful until he does appear?

There are those who believe the 'rapture' will take place at some time during the tribulation period. They are referred to as mid-tribulation believers. They state the church is referred to as being on the earth until the fourteenth chapter of Revelation, where it states: *"And I looked, and behold a white cloud, and upon the cloud one sat like unto the Son of man, having on his head a golden crown, and in his hand a sharp sickle. And another angel came out of the temple, crying with a loud voice to him that sat on the cloud. Thrust in thy sickle and reap; for the time is come for thee to reap; for the harvest of the earth is ripe."* *(Revelation 14:14-15)* There are those who allude to this verse: *"Behold, I come as a thief. Blessed is he that watches, and keeps his garments, lest he walk naked, and they see his shame."* *(Revelation 16:15)* They believe this is a clue the Lord will return somewhere during the time of the Great Tribulation, rather than before this period begins.

Then there is the reference to the ten virgins and the bridegroom in Matthew chapter 25, where the bridegroom is referred to returning at midnight. What wedding starts at midnight? Is God trying to tell us to prepare to go the distance?

The virgins who weren't prepared with enough oil, or did not anticipate the wedding would occur so late, tried to rush out to obtain more oil for their lamps, and the bridegroom arrived while they were out trying to get prepared at the last minute. Some interpret this to mean the Lord's return will not be at the beginning of this tribulation period, but somewhere in the middle.

Still others believe Christ will come at the end of the tribulation period, by looking at chapter 19 as a clue to the Lord's return, where it states: *"Let us be glad and rejoice, and give honor to him: for the marriage of the Lamb is come, and his wife hath made herself ready. And to her was granted that she should be arrayed in fine linen, clean and white; for the fine linen is the righteousness of saints...And he saith unto me, write, blessed are they which are called unto the marriage supper of the Lamb."* (Revelation 19:7-9 KJV) Those who believe this will happen long into the events of the great tribulation do not ignore the scripture concerning being saved from the wrath of God, but state God will 'cover' his children in his hand during this time, and keep them safe in the midst of it all. They take the events of Noah as an example, where God poured out his wrath on all the earth, but kept Noah and his family "hidden" in the ark, safe and sound.

In regards to this scripture, I remember many years ago while in prayer, the Lord gave me a beautiful experience. It was in the form of a vision or daydream. I saw this great throne, and seated on the throne was a cloud of light, so bright you could not see the image of who was in the cloud. The room was so large that it did not seem to have dimensions. There was a sea of people before this throne. Jesus was there, dressed in the most glorious white garments, and trimmed with gold. His face was so bright that I could not see his features clearly, but I knew it was him. He was looking toward the back of the enormous room. These huge golden doors in the back opened up, and a sea of people dressed in white, like brides, came in. I could see a smile on the Lord's face, a smile of complete love and joy. His bride, "the church", was being ushered into his presence. After a period of time, when all these saints dressed in white wedding gowns had all entered, Jesus turned toward the throne and said, "Father, this is my bride, who has been washed in my blood and made clean." There was a great rejoicing and songs of praise rang out. Then the vision or daydream ended, leaving me with such a feeling of joy; I wanted to shout! Was this a figment of my imagination? Some may think so, but I truly believe this was just a short glimpse into what we will one day experience in full, those of us who have chosen to serve him.

On another occasion, during one of my prayer times, I saw this glorious place again. I was in a huge corridor. I saw an enormous room with the doors open. As I looked in, I saw a table which went on and on. It was covered with the finest white linen, and set with gold place settings. There were beautiful flower centerpieces, and fine crystal goblets decorating this enormous table. Each chair at the table was unique. The seats were covered in fine fabric, but the frame of the chair had a gold overlay, which was ornamentally engraved. They each had a different symbol or image on the back which was engraved into the gold and on the top rim was a gold name plate. I remember seeing my name written on one of the chairs, and my heart jumped for joy. In an instant, a thought flashed across my mind to see if there were chairs with the names of my children there. I looked up, as if to search, but before I could look, God spoke to my heart and said, "All of your children have a place at this table." What an exhilarating feeling came over me! I am sharing this with you because I have spoken to so many mothers who are concerned for the salvation of their children. This vision has meant so much for my faith during the hard times in raising my children.

The word of God promises us in the book of Acts, "Believe in the Lord Jesus Christ, and you and your household will be saved." It also tells us in the book of Proverbs to "train up a child in the way that he should go, and when he is old he will not depart". These are precious promises given to all believers, to every concerned parent. This is not just a wishful thought, but promises made by God concerning the salvation of the children of the believer. Does this mean they are automatically saved, regardless of their actions? Not at all, but it is an assurance God will continue to lead our children, to convict them, and reach out to them in order to bring them to salvation. The seed of the Word of God we plant in their hearts when they are young, will remain there, and will at some time in their life, produce results. They may go far away from the ways of God, but God will continue to remind them of those words spoken into their hearts when they were young. He will continue to reach out to them to draw them back to his side. The scripture says the Word of God will not return void, but will accomplish the purpose it was sent out to accomplish. How long it takes doesn't matter; we as parents must hang on to these precious promises believing God, who promised, is faithful to fulfill his promises. It is because of his great love, and the promises in his Word, that my children will have a seat at the banquet table for the marriage supper of the lamb.

I became a Christian before I had my children. I remember dedicating my life, and the lives of whatever children the Lord would see fit to give me to his service. As each child was born, I would dedicate them to the Lord, and from the time they were born, I would tell them about the things of God. I took them to church, read them scriptures, taught them to pray, and told them they were born with a special purpose, to be a servant of God, in whatever way he chose for them to serve him. I followed what the Word of God said, to train up the child in the way he should go. Have any of them wandered off the path? Yes, but my faith in God's Word remains. I have seen each one of them confess Jesus as their Lord and Savior. They have not always followed him with their whole heart, but I take comfort knowing they are in the Lord's hands, and he will guide them on life's journey to where they are meant to be. To all of you who read this who are parents, I say, trust in the Lord, and put your children in God's hands, He will not fail your trust.

Now, regarding the different opinions about the Lord's return, I am not attempting to state which of these theories may be the correct one, because in truth, only the Father knows the time when Jesus will return. What I want to emphasize is the scriptural evidence which states **he will return**. Knowing the mystery as to when is not as important as our being ready whenever he returns. We should not allow this to bring debate and division in the church. We will find out when God chooses to reveal it. Until then, the church needs to be united in faith, in the promise he will return for us, and be busy preaching his message to the ends of earth, in order to prepare mankind for the eventful day. Regardless of which theory you choose to believe, one thing is evident, God will take care of his children, and he WILL return to take them with him.

The word of God gives us some clues as to the events which will occur on the earth as signs of his eminent return. Biblical experts agree events surrounding the nation of Israel are the most prophetically revealing signs. Most believe when Israel became a nation again, it was a signal indicating the 'final countdown' on God's prophetic clock. There are statements in the Bible in regards to Jerusalem being in the hand of the Jewish people and the temple having been re-built, at the time of his return. It is interesting to note Jewish religious leaders believe it is essential for the temple to be rebuilt in order for Messiah to come. They have made extensive preparations for the rebuilding of their temple and are waiting to proceed forward. I have heard testimonies of how they have been training the priesthood for the day they will be ministering to the people who come to the temple, following the ancient instructions written in the Torah concerning the priestly garments and rituals. There is a great search on their behalf to locate the Ark of the Covenant, and the Red Heifer without spot or blemish to sacrifice. The obstacle which prevents them from beginning this construction is the Islamic Mosque which is presently located on the ancient temple site. How this issue will be resolved, only God knows, but the Jewish people are looking towards the day God will somehow miraculously intervene and return this site to the hands of the Jews so they can begin to re-construct the temple. The book of Revelation, as well as the book of Daniel, makes reference to the Antichrist standing in the Holy temple, as a great abomination, which also seems to indicate the temple will be rebuilt as a sign of the end times, if you interpret it literally.

(There are those who believe this is a symbolic reference, and not a literal one.)

Let us avoid debate, the important issue is: Jesus will return! He made it clear though we may not know the day or the hour, there are some signs which will serve as a signal when his return is near. Here are some of the scriptures the Lord has given us as signs of his return to earth: *"But when ye shall hear of wars and commotions, be not terrified; for these things must first come to pass; but the end is not by and by"*. *Then said he unto them, "nation shall rise against nation, and kingdom against kingdom: and great earthquakes shall be in divers places, and famines, and pestilences; and fearful sights and great signs shall there be from heaven." (Luke 21: 9-11)* Clearly, there will a great distress among the nations. There will be evidence of the kingdom of God and the kingdom of the enemy coming into striking conflict. There will be a war of evil against what is good and right. Anything which refers to Christianity and the Word of God will be challenged, and an attempt to overthrow it will be waged by the followers of darkness. Even in the United States at this present time, there is an increase of debate over such issues as prayer in schools, scripture being used in public places, the right to life issues, challenges to God's structure for the family, even to the extent of displaying Christian symbols in public places. It seems as if the very word of God is on trial in a nation that professes to be a "Christian" nation. In the attempt to preserve freedom, there has been a misinterpretation of the intent of the founding fathers that formed this nation. We have been so legally consumed with what might offend or violate someone's rights, that our right to believe in Christ is being severely challenged and limited, while the right to follow anything else but the Word of God is given free reign. These issues are being used to 'educate' and influence future generations. This is one more reason, as parents, and grandparents, we must teach our children what the Word of God says, because sadly, they are not often receiving Godly instruction in their schools. I believe this is a sign of 'kingdom rising against kingdom'. The kingdom of God is definitely being attacked.

The scripture also refers to some natural events which will signal the approach of the end times. It seems as if the spiritual war for the souls of men will spill over into nature, and result in God's creation crying out for man to stop and consider God before it's too late. There will be an increase in natural disasters upon the earth, and signs, or celestial events which will occur in the heavens. Jesus said: *"And there shall be signs in the sun, and in the moon, and in the stars; and upon the earth distress of nations, with perplexity; the sea and the waves roaring: Men's hearts failing them for fear, and for looking after those things which are coming on the earth: for the powers of heaven shall be shaken. And then shall they see the Son of man coming in the clouds with power and great glory."* *(Luke 21:25-27 KJV)* There will be great signs of distress among the nations, confusion and fear gripping the hearts of men because of all of the things happening on the earth at once! There will be mighty tidal waves, and the earth will be shaken in different places all over the world. It sounds like something out of the headlines which we have read in this past decade. Scientists have stated they have seen a dramatic increase in earthquakes in the last twenty years or so. We see terrorist attacks, as religious extremist war against those of different faiths. There have been great famines in parts of Africa, which have cost the lives of thousands upon thousands. Not to mention the AIDS epidemic claiming so many lives or the outbreak of different plagues (viruses and diseases). The increase in people dying of heart attacks is astounding. They have pointed to all types of causes, but most doctors agree a common underlying fact is the effect of stress on the body. The economic situation seems to have worsened, causing even more panic and stress. Great hurricanes, great earthquakes, multiple tornadoes touching down, the rise of suicide, the increase child abusers and murderers, are all signs of the approaching day of the Lord.

Recorded in the book of Matthew, the Lord said: *"Immediately after the distress of those days the sun will be darkened, and the moon will not give its light; the stars will fall from the sky, and the heavenly bodies will be shaken. At that time the sign of the Son of man will appear in the sky: and all the nations of the earth will mourn. They will see the Son of man coming on the clouds of the sky, with power and great glory. And he will send his angels with a loud trumpet call, and they will gather his elect from the four winds, from one end of the heavens to the other. Now learn the lesson of the fig tree: as soon as its twigs get tender, and its leaves come out, you know that summer is near. Even so, when you see all these things, you know that it (or he) is near, right at the door. I tell you the truth, this generation will certainly not pass away, until all these have happened."* (Matthew 24:29-35 NIV) He tells us to look for the signs, and states the generation who begins to see these signs will see the coming of the Lord. Accordingly, the generation who sees all these things happen will not end before all the things written in the scripture are fulfilled. Could we be that generation?

These events were also revealed to Isaiah the prophet: *"Wail, for the day of the Lord is near; it will come like destruction from the Almighty. Because of this, all hands go limp; every man's heart will melt. Terror will seize them; pain and anguish will grip them; they will writhe like a woman in labor. They will look aghast at each other, their faces aflame. See the day of the Lord is coming, a cruel day, with wrath and fierce anger, to make the land desolate and he shall destroy the sinners within it. The stars of heaven and the constellations will not show their light. The rising sun will be darkened, and the moon will not give its light. I will punish the world for its evil, the wicked for their sins. I will put an end to the arrogance of the haughty and will humble the pride of the ruthless. " (Isaiah 13:6-11 NIV)* Further prophecy concerning the signs of the end of this sinful age appear in the book of Joel as well: *"The earth shall quake before them; the heavens shall tremble: the sun and the moon shall be dark, and the stars shall withdraw their shining; And the Lord shall utter his voice before his army; for his camp is very great: for he is strong that executes his word: for the day of the Lord is great and very terrible: and who can abide it?" (Joel 2:10-11 KJV) "And I will show wonders in the heavens and in the earth, blood, and fire, and pillars of smoke. The sun shall be turned into darkness, and the moon into blood, before the terrible day of the Lord come. And it shall come to pass, that whosoever shall call on the name of the Lord shall be delivered: for in mount Zion and in Jerusalem shall be deliverance, as the Lord hath said, and in the remnant whom the Lord shall call." (Joel 2:30-32 KJV)*

These terrible warnings to the inhabitants of the earth, also contains a beautiful promise to whoever will call on the name of the Lord, the promise of deliverance! These scriptures also confirm many of the details written in the book of Revelation. Jesus compared these days to the wickedness which was wide spread in the days of Noah, when people had also rejected the knowledge of God. They were totally taken up with the pleasures of the flesh, eating, drinking, marrying, as if it was all there was to life. They were an egocentric society who did whatever seemed right in their own eyes; God was not a consideration for them. Unfortunately, we can see this prevailing attitude in society today. This is another sign we may be in the days when Christ will return. As in the days of Noah, people oblivious to what was about to happen, is this generation just as blind to what may happen suddenly? The scriptures tells us: *"Now brothers, about times and dates we have no need to write to you, for you know very well that the day of the Lord will come like a thief in the night. While people are saying "peace and safety", destruction will come upon them suddenly, as labor pains on a pregnant woman, and they will not escape. But you brothers are not in darkness, that this day should surprise you like a thief."* (I Thessalonians 5:1-4 NIV)

God has warned us of these events and what is going to take place upon the earth ahead of time. He has showed us his plan for redemption, and given us this promise: "whosoever calls upon the name of the Lord shall be saved." For this reason we should rejoice because our names are written down in the book of life, and because we have God's promise we will escape the wrath of God poured out over all those on the earth who have hated him and rejected his ways. But it should also instill in us a sense of urgency to reach others with the good news of God's plan to forgive sins and save man. God loves people so much that he sent his Son to die for them. He tells us to love others, as Christ has loved us, and yet, so many who say they love the Lord, don't seem to be concerned about the fate of others. We can get so busy in the day to day affairs of our lives, that we don't take time to share Jesus with others.

114

We think we have all the time in the world to share what Jesus means to us, so we put off for tomorrow, what we should be doing today.

This reminds me of an incident which occurred with one of my sons. He stood in a pulpit at graduation and told the story of a young student from his school that was always a bit odd. He was a sullen kid, a bit gothic in appearance, who never seemed to mingle with anyone or have many friends. My son was never rude to him; he didn't make fun of him like others had, and he hoped one day the opportunity would arise where he might be able to share Jesus with this young man. He thought he had time. He wept before the crowd listening on that day, for this young man suddenly committed suicide, and he never did get the chance to share Jesus with him. He was grieved over the fact he never took time to talk to this young man about Christ. How many of us can say the same thing? There was someone, a neighbor, an old school friend, a brother or sister, a parent, someone we saw standing on the corner with their hand held out, who we conveniently avoided eye contact with, people who we could have said something to, should have said something to, but didn't. If you have Jesus in your heart, you have a treasure, hidden inside you. You have the hope of mankind inside you. People are searching for the answer, and there you are, standing with the answer hidden inside you! Sadly, we have all missed these precious moments, opportunities God gives us, to touch a life with God's love.

If we truly love his appearing, if we want to be with him, how can we not share this love, this passion with others? People talk about the things which mean the most to them. Women talk about their children, men talk about their jobs, about sports, about whatever they truly care about. Just run into a new grandparent, and they will pull out the pictures of their precious grandchild and tell you all about them! People talk about what is most important to them. The Bible say:"out of the abundance of the heart, the mouth speaks". This is a good measuring stick to judge how our relationship with him is going. What do you spend most of your waking moments thinking about? What comes to your mind when someone asks what is most important to you, or what your passion in life is? There may be a lot of things which come to mind, but if Jesus isn't at the top of the list, it's time to do some soul searching. All of the blessings I have received in my life, my husband, my children, my health, my home, all of these are gifts given by a loving God. How can I love the gifts more than the giver? If you aren't sharing this love for Christ, this passion, it's a good time to reflect as to why not. Perhaps you felt it once, but you've let the flame flicker, other priorities have quenched your passion, or perhaps you have never had a real one on one encounter with Jesus. Maybe you know a great deal ABOUT him, but you don't really KNOW him! I hope this book will help you to know him in a personal, life changing way, which you will want to share with others.

In conclusion as to the return of our Lord Jesus, regardless of how you interpret the scriptures, the signs of the end, whether literal or figuratively, the underlying message is his promise to return. The importance should be placed on the fact he will return, and what we are doing in the meantime. If we believe, our actions will correspond to our beliefs. I want to be found "watching and waiting", as the scripture says. I believe this means to be prepared for whatever time it occurs. I also believe it means to be responsible to carry on the work of the Kingdom with urgency, until he comes, because we don't know the day or the hour.

CHAPTER TEN
THE GREAT TRIBULATION

The Bible refers to a time when there will be such tribulation on the earth, like man has never seen before. This is hard for us to imagine when we think of the horrible atrocities which have taken place over the history of man, the dark ages, the inquisition, the holocaust, world wars, mass genocide in different areas of the earth, how could it possibly be any worse? The scripture describes a time when an evil force will rise to stamp out the Saints of God and the Word of God, like in no other time. This force is found in the person referred to as the Antichrist. There are those who believe this is a literal person who will arise; others believe it refers to a government system more than an individual. Regardless of interpretation, it is the evil of Satan himself, in his last attempt to destroy God and his people. Satan is aware his time is running out. He knows the final judgment against him will come, and so he will strike back with a ferocious last effort.

First of all, let's take a look at the description of 'antichrist';

literally the word means to be anti, or against Christ; the 'antichrist' is the direct opposite of Christ. He is an enemy of the Messiah, who will try to imitate Christ, in order to deceive mankind into worshiping him. The word antichrist is listed in the Bible in the epistles of John: *"Little children, it is the last time: and as ye have heard that antichrist shall come, even now are there many antichrists; whereby we know that it is the last time." (I John 2:18)* John goes on to explain what an antichrist spirit is by saying, *"Who is a liar but he that denies that Jesus is the Christ? He is antichrist that denies the Father and the Son." (I John 2:22 KJV)* He continues to give light into identifying such a spirit by saying, *"And every spirit that confesses not that Jesus Christ is come in the flesh is not of God: and this is that spirit of antichrist, whereof ye have heard that it should come; and even now already is it in the world." (I John 4:3 KJV)* This might lead one to think that John believed the coming of the Lord was during his lifetime and the antichrist was alive already, however, in the following verse it states any deceiver who does not confess Jesus has come in the flesh is an 'antichrist'. *"For many deceivers are entered into the world, who confess not that Jesus Christ is come in the flesh. This is a deceiver and an antichrist." (2 John 1:7 KJV)* Throughout history we have seen this antichrist spirit inhabiting different leaders. Those who rise to power and use the power to try to destroy Christianity are all types of 'antichrist'.

Paul describes this antichrist spirit further, referring to him as 'the son of perdition.' *"Don't let anyone deceive you in any way, for that day will not come until the rebellion occurs and the man of lawlessness is revealed (the son of perdition), the man doomed to destruction. He will oppose and will exalt himself over everything that is called God, or is worshiped, so that he sets himself up in God's temple, proclaiming himself to be God. Don't you remember, when I was with you, I used to tell you these things? And now you know what is holding him back, so that he may be revealed at the proper time. For the secret power of lawlessness is already at work; but the one who now holds it back will continue to do so till he is taken out of the way. And the lawless one will be revealed whom the Lord Jesus will overthrow with the breath of his mouth and destroy by the splendor of his coming. The coming of the lawless one will be in accordance with the work of Satan displayed in all kinds of counterfeit miracles, signs and wonders, and in every sort of evil that deceives those who are perishing. They perish because they refused to love the truth and be saved." (II Thessalonians 2:4-10 NIV)*

This description gives us a deeper look into the nature and motive of this spirit. It wants to take the place of God, to sit on God's throne and be worshiped by man as if he were God. He wants to rise above God and have the adoration and worship which only God deserves! It matches the description we see of Lucifer when he fell; he was prideful and rebellious, jealous of God to the point of trying to usurp his power and place. This is a clue for us to recognize such a man (or system), a person (or government) who wants power above all else, and to be adored by all.

Jesus warned us of those who will try to pass themselves off as 'the Christ': *"For there shall arise false Christs, and false prophets, and shall shew great signs and wonders; insomuch that, if it were possible, they shall deceive the very elect."* *(Matthew 24:24 KJV)* These 'Christ impersonators' try to deceive by attempting to duplicate some of the miracles which Christ performed, in an attempt to deceive even those who are believers. The disguise will be quite a convincing one for those who are not led by the Spirit of God, but the Holy Spirit will reveal the truth to all those who truly believe. The antichrist personality is extremely charismatic, with great ability to flatter and impress. This spirit will attempt to fool the religious people of this world into believing he is their messiah. Once he has gained adulation and power, he will reveal his true nature by attempting to destroy anyone who recognizes who he really is, and refuses to submit to him; *"And it was given unto him to make war with the saints, and to overcome them: and power was given him over all kindreds, and tongues, and nations. And all that dwell upon the earth shall worship him, whose names are not written in the book of life of the Lamb slain from the foundation of the world." (Revelation 13:7-8 KJV)*

The Bible seems to imply this is a person, a man who is taken by this spirit, but there are those who believe it more widely implies a government system. Regardless of interpretation, there are some signs we can observe. The Bible tells us this antichrist will receive a mortal wound, but miraculously survive. It implies it is a physical wound to the head, which some argue is symbolic of a wound to its power or leadership. Nevertheless, the scripture indicates this wound will be healed miraculously, deceiving many into believing this man is truly of God. A second 'beast' will arise and do great signs and wonders as well; he is often referred to as the false prophet. Some believe this is a religion or religious leader who carries a great amount of power over the population. This false prophet will cause all men to worship the image of the beast, or the antichrist.

The Bible describes these times, as a time when mankind will be forced to receive a 'mark' given to them by this beast in either their right hand or upon their foreheads, without which, they will not be able to buy or sell anything. The clue is given that the number of this beast is six hundred threescore and six, or '666'. *"And I beheld another beast coming up out of the earth; and he exercises all the power of the first beast before him, and causes the earth and them which dwell therein to worship the first beast, whose deadly wound was healed. And he does great wonders, so that he makes fire come down from heaven on the earth in the sight of men. And deceives them that dwell on the earth by the means of those miracles which he had power to do in the sight of the beast; saying to them that dwell on the earth, that they should make an image to the beast which had the wound by a sword and did live. And he had power to give life unto the image of the beast, that the image of the beast should both speak, and cause that as many as would not worship the image of the beast should be killed. And he causes all, both small and great, rich and poor, free and bond, to receive a mark in their right hand, or in their foreheads: And that no man might buy or sell, save he that had the mark, or the name of the beast, or the number of his name. Here is wisdom. Let him that has understanding count the number of the beast: for it is the number of a man; and his number is six hundred threescore and six."* (Revelation 13:11-18)

There has been a lot of speculation as to what the number means. Some have thought it is a literal way to calculate the name of the person, others believe it is more symbolic of a system or government, controlled by numbers, and point to the universal bar code system which has been placed on all packaged items we now purchase, as a possible clue of this antichrist system. Others believe he is a literal man, stating the number six is symbolic of man, since God made man on the sixth day. There is so much speculation and theories on this subject. Again, as with the timing of the rapture, the Bible states it is a mystery which will be revealed when he, who keeps it hidden, chooses to reveal it, in other words, the Spirit of God will reveal the interpretation as to who this person or system is when the time comes. God has given us a character description in order for us to be able to identify such potential candidates, but more importantly, he warns us not to follow after men, especially those who are consumed with themselves, no matter the great words they might speak, or how sincere they may sound. We must be careful of those who crave power, and use it for their own personal gains. For those who oppose the antichrist, it will be terrible times. He will kill all those who refuse to bow down to him. Those who choose to serve Jesus will be persecuted and become martyrs. All of this is the devils last attempt to stamp out Christianity and defeat the Son of God, but the scripture tells us Christ will return to put down this insurrection.

The period in which the antichrist will reign is referred to in the Bible as a time of great tribulation, such as the world has never seen. During this time, God will pour out his wrath upon the earth. There will be hail, earthquakes, volcanic activity, and what some believe appears to be a meteor or asteroid which will fall to earth and cause massive destruction. There will be great plagues and pestilences which will fall on mankind. This is a time of judgment over evil men who rejected God's plan to save them through Jesus Christ. The word of God states at that time men will hide for fear, and will seek death, and not find it.

This is a horrible time for mankind, and only those who turn to Christ will be saved.

There are those who do not believe in a literal tribulation period, but believe the book of Revelation is a book which was specific to events during the age of the first church. There are others who believe this book is an overall history of the church from beginning to end; still others believe it is a book which is set in the future and its events will unfold at the end of the age, when Christ returns. There are so many varied opinions regarding the Lord's return and the rapture of the church, it would take a whole book to list them all, and frankly, it would be of little benefit. While holding sound doctrine is important to the mission of the church, we must hold fast to what we do know, not what we speculate to be true. We know Jesus is Lord. We know he died for our sins and rose again. We know he is returning. These are the truths we must remain constant about. Future details described in the word of God are shrouded in a veil. Everyone's interpretation is not the same. The only true authority on what each detail means is God himself. Faith is trusting God when you can't clearly see, or when you don't understand it all. Those who like to engage themselves in philosophical debate might not agree, but this book is not an attempt to explain everything, it is meant to reveal the heart of God and his eternal plan for us.

Regardless of which point of view one might have, the scripture lets us know it is a time of great turmoil, compared to a woman giving birth, with great pains as she labors to bring a new life into the world. In truth, the old, sinful world is about to give way to the deliverance of the world, where Jesus Christ will reign in every heart for eternity, and all his enemies will be under his feet.

The events, described throughout the Bible referring to these end times, are difficult to interpret, and they are frightening. The time of this tribulation culminates in a final battle waged when the kings of the earth come together, described as the battle of Armageddon. *"And I saw three unclean spirits like frogs come out of the mouth of the dragon, and out of the mouth of the beast, and out of the mouth of the false prophet. For they are the spirits of devils, working miracles, which go forth unto the kings of the earth and of the whole world, to gather them to the battle of that great day of God Almighty...And he gathered them together into a place called in the Hebrew tongue Armageddon. And the seventh angel poured out his vial into the air; and there came a great voice out of the temple of heaven, from the throne, saying, it is done."* (Revelation 16:14; 16 KJV) The book of Isaiah tells of this event as follows: *"I have commanded my sanctified ones; I have also called my mighty ones for mine anger, even them that rejoice in my highness. The noise of a multitude in the mountains, like as of a great people; the tumultuous noise of the kingdoms of nations gathered together: the Lord of Hosts musters the host of the battle. They come from a far country, from the end of heaven, even the Lord, and the weapons of his indignation, to destroy the whole land."* (Isaiah 13:3-5 KJV)

The book of Revelation tells us in detail the outcome of this great battle: *"And I saw heaven opened, and behold a white horse; and he that sat upon him was called Faithful and True, and in righteousness he does judge and make war. His eyes were as a flame of fire, and on his head were many crowns; and he had a name written that no man knew, but he himself. And he was clothed with vesture dipped in blood: and his name is called the Word of God. And the armies which were in heaven followed him upon white horses, clothed in fine linen, white and clean...And I saw the beast, and the kings of the earth, and their armies, gathered together to make war against him that sat on the horse and his army. And the beast was taken, and with him the false prophet that wrought miracles before him, with which he deceived them that received the mark of the beast, and them that worshiped his image. These both were cast alive into a lake of fire burning with brimstone. And the remnants were slain with the sword of him that sat upon the horse, which sword proceeded out of his mouth; and all the fowls were filled with their flesh." (Revelation 19:11-14; 19-21 KJV)*

The outcome is told! Those who rebelled against God and persecuted God's children will be defeated! The Lord himself will come, with the host of heaven, to fight against the antichrist and his false prophet, against all the devil's forces, and they will be defeated. We who believe, who have remained faithful to Christ, will witness this great defeat. I can't imagine the shout of victory which will sound, and then, an even greater shout will be heard when the Lord will bind the devil with a great chain and cast him into the bottomless pit: *"And I saw an angel come down from heaven, having the key of the bottomless pit and a great chain in his hand. And he laid hold on the dragon, that old serpent, which is the Devil, and Satan, and bound him a thousand years. And cast him into the bottomless pit, and shut him up, and set a seal upon him, that he should deceive the nations no more, till the thousand years should be fulfilled; and after that he must be loosed a little season." (Revelation 20:1-3 KJV)*

Jesus won the victory on the cross, and he will demonstrate it to all on that day! The victory is ours! All of the saints in heaven, all of the angels, all of us who have believed and remained faithful will get to witness this victorious moment. I have heard about the great celebration which occurred at the end of World War II. I heard bells went off all over, and people ran into the streets to hug each other and celebrate. Everyone stopped to celebrate the victory, the war was over. Well, this will be an event which will completely overshadow that day. It won't just be a victory for America, but for the whole world, for believers from all generations, from all nations. Heaven and earth will sound off with shouts of victory, bells ringing, people singing, angels praising, we are going to have some celebration! Don't get caught up in trying to understand the time line of events and details so much it distracts from the focus of the final outcome. Will we be taken in the rapture and go to heaven and then seven years later return with the Lord for the final battle? Or does it happen we are caught up to join him as his armies are coming for this final event? Will we be here, or will we be there? There is so much debate and difference of opinion over these things, but what is important is we will be with HIM, with JESUS, forevermore. Wherever he goes, that's where we will be. The mystery as to how this will actually happen only God knows, and since our time on earth is measured in minutes, what may seem like an instant in heaven, could seem like years to those on earth. Don't get confused or bogged down trying to decipher all the details or hidden meanings. You don't need to know how God made the sun in order to know it will shine each day, and you don't need to know how he is going to do all he has promised in order to believe he will bring it to pass. I know he is coming back for me; I know regardless of how or when, I will be with him forever, and nothing will ever be able to separate us. That's the desire of his heart and mine. I am hanging on to this truth by faith, and anxiously awaiting the day, are you?

CHAPTER ELEVEN
THE MILLENNIUM

The Bible refers to a time period after the Lord overthrows the forces of Satan and brings peace to the earth for one thousand years as the Millennium. According to what is stated in scripture, after the great battle where the nations who come against Israel are defeated by Christ and his heavenly army, Satan will be bound and thrown into a bottomless pit for a thousand years. There is also a reference eluding that after the thousand years have passed apparently Satan will be released again for a short time. The Bible doesn't state why he will be released, or how many days or months the "short time" will actually be. One can only speculate the reason for this apparent "reprieve". Only God knows the reason for this, but we can be certain whatever the reason, it is to achieve his ultimate purpose for mankind, which is good.

What will it be like on earth during this thousand year period? Who will be there? There are many different opinions on this subject as well. Some theorize all believers will live during this time, citing those God has chosen to rule and reign over the nations will be there to do so. Others believe only those who came out of the great tribulation as martyrs will be on earth. The Bible states: *"I saw thrones on which were seated those who had been given authority to judge. And I saw the souls of those who had been beheaded because of their testimony for Jesus and because of the Word of God. They had not worshiped the beast or his image and had not received his mark on their foreheads or their hands. They came to life and reigned with Christ for a thousand years. (The rest of the dead did not come to life until the thousand years were ended.) This is the first resurrection. Blessed and holy are those who have part in the first resurrection. The second death has no power over them, but they will be priests of God and of Christ and will reign with him for a thousand years."* (Revelation 20:4-6 NIV) This scripture seems to imply there are those who lived in the tribulation period who were faithful to God and did not receive the mark of the beast, and as their reward, these martyrs of the Tribulation period, will come to life again and reign with Christ during this period. It is understandable why some believe this indicates only these martyrs will reign on the earth during the Millennium period. However, there are those who say, the ones seated on the thrones who were given authority to judge are believers, and they will also reign with the martyrs during the Millennium period. Their reasoning is that the believers are not in danger of the second death either. They too are part of the faithful who serve Christ, and the second death, (eternal separation from God) has no power over them. Plus there is the scriptural reference of the promises to them, which are stated at the beginning of the book of Revelation: *"He that overcomes will not be hurt at all by the second death"* (Revelation 2:11 NIV); *"To him who overcomes and does my will to the end, I*

will give authority over the nations." (Revelation 2:26 NIV)
"They will be priests of God and of Christ and will reign with
him for a thousand years", if interpreted literally appear to
indicate that Christ will reign over the earth during this period
along with his priests.

There are others who believe the millennium period is a
symbolic period of time, which refers to a spiritual time of
Christ reigning, from the victory on the cross forward, along
with those whom he established his kingdom within, more than
a literal thousand year period. They believe the Kingdom that
the Word refers to is the Spiritual Kingdom of God reigning on
earth rather than a literal Kingdom. They reference how the
Jews in the time of Jesus failed to understand the spiritual
messages the Lord spoke referred to an eternal Kingdom, not a
literal one. The Jewish leaders were disappointed when Jesus
did not establish a literal kingdom, overthrowing the Roman
Empire. They believe the references to the Kingdom of God
being established in Revelation is in the spiritual realm, within
in the hearts of men, rather than physically upon the earth.
Either way one may interpret the scriptures, the truth is that
both thoughts have merit, and scriptural backing, but perhaps it
may mean both literal and spiritual. The interpretation of the
book of Revelation is the subject of much debate because it is
mysterious. Only God knows the exact interpretation. All our
theories and interpretations are the conclusion of personal
opinions. Can something that begins in the Spiritual realm be
completed in the physical realm at some point? Of course it can.
God created all that was created in his own thought, in the
spiritual realm first, and then he spoke it into the physical
realm, making it a physical reality. The Kingdom Jesus
established when he said it was finished, was completed on the

Cross, and established in every believer when they accept him into their heart. His Kingdom is established in the heart of every believer who surrenders their life to him, and lives their life for him. Where the King is, there is his Kingdom. If we invite him into our hearts, his kingdom is established there, where he is. The Spiritual Kingdom of God on earth already is. He lives and exists through his people, carrying out his will on earth, as it is in heaven. Will the spiritual kingdom which now is on earth one day see the physical manifestation of his kingdom physically coming down to earth as well? Many believe this is what the scripture states, and whether you believe it is to be taken literally or not, the most important thing to remember is everything belongs to the Lord, and however he chooses to fulfill the scriptures referring to him and his kingdom are entirely up to him. The important thing is that he is the King of Kings, and his kingdom is an eternal kingdom, home to all who have believed and followed him. We will be with him forever! What else matters?

Peter refers to the believer as being "a chosen people, a royal priesthood" in I Peter 2:9. The book of Revelation states when none were found to open the book then came forth a spotless lamb, Jesus: *"You are worthy to take the scroll and to open its seals, because you were slain, and with your blood you purchased men for God from every tribe and language and people and nation. You have made them to be a kingdom and priests to serve our God, and they will reign on the earth"* *(Revelation 5:9-10 NIV) These* scriptures seem to imply his people will reign on the earth, referring to all believers, not just those who came out of the tribulation period, during the Millennium period. Still some believe there are scriptures which refer to the church being in heaven, having been "caught up with the Lord", and present at the marriage supper of the Lamb. There are scriptural references such as the passage in the book of Revelation which states: *"Him who overcomes I will make a pillar in the temple of my God. Never again will he leave it. I will write on him the name of my God and the name of the city of my God, the New Jerusalem, which is coming down out of heaven from my God." (Revelation 3:12 NIV)* This scripture seems to confirm that latter belief, yet it also states that the city, the New Jerusalem, is coming down from heaven.

I am not attempting to prove or disprove either set of beliefs; both have their scriptural basis, and such debates serve little purpose other than bringing division in the body of Christ. I have made mention of several different beliefs held in the body of Christ, with the purpose to inform. Undoubtedly, there are many more theories out there, which many of you may have heard. My purpose in addressing some of them is to emphasize there will always be differences in thought, but they should not bring divisions among us. God never intended these clues to "divide" his body. He made us aware of these clues in order for us to trust in him for the understanding and for the unfolding of the mystery. Does it really matter whether we are here or there, as long as we are in God's kingdom? We should focus more on the souls of those who will not be part of his kingdom unless we reach them with the good news of Jesus Christ.

This book is to bring to light the wonderful things God has told us about his plan and about his Kingdom. The Bible says, *"No eye has seen, no ear has heard, no mind has conceived what God has prepared for those who love him." (I Corinthians 2:9 NIV)* In other words, it is unimaginable! I can only imagine the marvels God has created for us in his heaven. On one occasion, while in prayer, the Lord showed me a vision of a wonderful place. I saw a garden which seemed to change as I went through it. First it was tropical in appearance, and then it was a beautiful rolling meadow, with enormous trees and flowers. I realized it had the different aspects of places I had seen on earth, but to a greater intensity and beauty than I have ever seen on earth. Isn't it amazing no matter where you grew up, no matter where you called "home", in heaven, you will feel right at "home"? If you came from a tropical country, it's there! If you came from the northern countries, where there are beautiful seasons, and great shady trees, it's there too! Isn't it just like God to have something special for every one of his children to enjoy, making us all feel at home in his kingdom?

I saw this beautiful wall, and inside was a great city. The streets were made of gold, and there were mansions which lined the streets. The amazing thing was each mansion was completely different from the other. The windows of these mansions were made up of solid precious stones. Can you imagine a precious stone the size of a bay window? Whether you believe this was just part of my imagination working overtime or not, this prayer experience changed me. I caught a glimpse of my heavenly home, and nothing on earth could compare. The things of this world suddenly didn't seem so important to me anymore. My desire to have a home, to buy nice things, diminished. I realized the things in this life are temporal, but my heavenly home was far greater, and I would spend eternity there. For years, the remembrance of those things God showed me brought me comfort and strength during hard times. I couldn't prove what I saw was real and not a figment of my imagination, but I believed God had given me a glimpse of what awaits those who are faithful to him. Then one day I came across a scripture which verified what I had seen. In the book of Isaiah it says, *"And I will make your windows of agates"*. *(Isaiah 54:12 KJV)* I had only ever read this in the King James Version, and I didn't know what agates were. When I read this same scripture in the Spanish Bible, it says literally, "and I will make your windows of precious stones." I hadn't realized an agate was a precious stone! When I read this, I realized what God had shown me several years before really was a revelation from him, confirmed in his word! I often think on this heavenly place and give thanks to God for giving me a "glimpse" of the other side.

Heaven is filled with so many marvelous things. The scripture tells us of a great throne, of angelic beings, of saints dressed in white, and the most beautiful praise ever heard being sung before the throne. It tells us his presence is so brilliant, so glorious; there is no need for any other source of light. Just hold a crystal or a prism up to the sun and watch the beams of beautiful colors streaming through, then imagine it multiplied a million times over! Even this does not compare to the glory of the Lord! I have heard stories of several people who died and had after-life experiences. One told of a place where the flowers were every color imaginable, and they swayed back and forth in praise. Another spoke of passing by trees filled with fruit which were the largest they had ever seen, and just the thought of tasting the fruit, brought the taste of it to your mouth. Another said whatever you wanted to do, or wherever you wanted to be, all you had to do was think of it, and you were suddenly there. All I can say at this point is "wow!" The one thing most of these experiences had in common was a sense of great joy and peace, and the desire to remain there and not return. God's grace has allowed us to have the technology to revive people, and to hear of their wonderful stories about what awaits us on the other side. Many have stated they saw a "bright light" which they were drawn to; others say the light was Jesus. The Bible states that Jesus is the way, the only way to our heavenly Father. It also states heaven will have no need of sun or moon or stars, for Jesus is the light there.

Heaven is a magnificent place! It doesn't get any better than to be in heaven in the presence of God! When we look at the terrible judgment coming on the earth during the Tribulation period, no one in their right mind would want to remain on earth and forego heaven. As for the Millennium period, there are scriptures which reveal some of the details of this period: *"And a highway will be there; it will be called the Way of Holiness. The unclean will not journey on it; it will be for those who walk in that Way; wicked fools will not go about on it. No lion will be there, neither will any ferocious beast get up on it; they will not be found there. But only the redeemed will walk there, and the ransomed of the Lord will return. They will enter Zion with singing; everlasting joy will crown their heads. Gladness and joy will overtake them, and sorrow and sighing will flee away."* (Isaiah 35:8-10 NIV) *"The wolf will live with the lamb, the leopard will lay down with the goat, the calf and the lion and the yearling together; and a little child will lead them. The cow will feed with the bear, their young will lie down together, and the lion will eat straw like the ox. The infant will play near the hole of the cobra, and the young child put his hand into the viper's nest. They will neither harm nor destroy on all my holy mountain, for the earth will be full of the knowledge of the Lord as the waters cover the sea." (Isaiah 11:6-9 NIV)*

The Bible describes it as a time of restoration for Israel. The promise God declared, to make Israel a praise among the nations, will be fulfilled, as seen in the following scripture: *"In the last days, the mountain of the Lord's temple will be established as chief among the mountains; it will be raised above the hills, and all nations will stream into it. Many peoples will come and say, "Come let us go up to the mountain of the Lord, to the house of the God of Jacob. He will teach us his ways, so that we may walk in his paths." The law will go out from Zion, the word of the Lord from Jerusalem. He will judge between the nations and will settle disputes for many peoples. They will beat their swords into plowshares and their spears into pruning hooks. Nation will not take up sword against nation, nor will they train for war anymore." (Isaiah 2:2-5 NIV)* There will be no more wars! All mankind, all of God's creation, will be at peace! Some believe these scriptures refer not to the time of the Millennium period, but to the time after God creates a new heaven and a new earth, as seen in Isaiah 65:17-25: *"Behold, I will create new heavens and a new earth. The former things will not be remembered, nor will they come to mind. But be glad and rejoice forever in what I will create, for I will create Jerusalem to be a delight and its people a joy. I will rejoice over Jerusalem and take delight in my people; the sound of weeping and of crying will be heard in it no more. Never again will there be in it an infant that lives but a few days, or an old man who does not live out his years; he who dies at a hundred will be thought a mere youth; he who fails to reach a hundred will be considered accursed. They will build houses and dwell in them; they will plant vineyards and eat their fruit. No longer will they build houses and others live in them, or plant and others eat. For as the days of a tree, so will be the days of my people; my chosen ones will long enjoy the work of their hands. They will not toil in vain or bear children doomed in misfortune; for they will be a people blessed by the Lord, they and their descendants with them. Before they call, I will answer; while they are still speaking, I will hear. The wolf and the lamb will feed together, and the lion will eat straw like the ox, but dust will be the serpent's food. They will neither harm nor destroy on all my holy mountain. "* However, in looking at this scripture, it mentions those who die will die of extreme old age, and other scriptures seem to indicate when God creates a new heaven and a new earth, death will not exist any longer. For this reason, this scripture is most commonly associated as prophetic of the Millennium kingdom.

The truth of the matter is we don't know exactly how, when, or why these prophetic events fit together, or play out. Which text refers to a certain period, or if part refers to one time, and another part refers to another time, is unclear. It is for this reason I continue to stress the importance of what these scriptures state over the importance of understanding all the details. Look at what the book of Isaiah states; Jerusalem will finally be at peace! There will not be war; there will not be any type of destruction, not even among animals, but the greatest of all is God will delight in his people! He will be one with them, answering their questions before they even speak. People will not have to work by the sweat of their brow to scratch out a living; they will not live in danger of losing their possessions. Doesn't this sound like going back to Eden? We can see God's plan to bring man back to how he had originally created him to be, in communion with him, with every need supplied by God. What a long journey mankind has taken. What a far path he has traveled away from God, but what a marvelous plan God has had, since the beginning, to restore all things, through Jesus Christ.

There are not many other details about this thousand year period. Some scriptures may refer to this period, or may apply to the time of the new heaven and new earth. In unraveling the mysteries of prophecy, we only have glimpses, clues, puzzle pieces, but the full picture still remains to be revealed. It is as if God is creating this wonderful banquet, and has let us "taste", but we can't fully enjoy or appreciate it to the fullest until it's time to sit down at the table. However, we can see from the "glimpses" it is all good, and we have a lot to look forward to.

Returning to the end of this thousand year period, as previously stated, the scripture states the devil will be released from the bottomless pit for a short time. He will once again go out to deceive the nations. Revelation states: *"When the thousand years are over, Satan will be released from his prison and will go out to deceive the nations in the four corners of the earth-Gog and Magog-to gather them for battle. In number they are like the sand of the seashore. They marched across the breadth of the earth and surrounded the camp of God's people, the city he loves. But fire came down from heaven and devoured them. And the devil, who deceived them, was thrown into the lake of burning sulfur, where the beast and the false prophet had been thrown. They will be tormented day and night forever."* (Revelation 20:7-10 NIV) Is the thousand years symbolic or literal? Is this a recount of another prophetic event previously written? Is this a referral to the time between when Christ triumphed over the kingdom of Satan two thousand years ago, and the period we are living in until he returns? If this is the case, why does it refer to Satan being thrown into the lake where the beast and the false prophet HAD been thrown? There are more questions than answers to all this, but let us return our focus to what is important, JESUS is the victor! Regardless of how it all happens or what it all means, our God wins! The Devil will get his dues; he will be thrown into the lake of fire, never to torment mankind again! Perhaps the information of this event playing out is sketchy for a reason, so Satan won't know exactly how or when it will happen, which may be part of his punishment.

CHAPTER TWELVE
THE GREAT WHITE THRONE JUDGMENT

The Bible states there is a time of final judgment for all mankind referred to as the Great White Throne Judgment: *"Then I saw a great white throne and him who was seated on it. Earth and sky fled from his presence, and there was no place for them. And I saw the dead, great and small, standing before the throne, and books were opened. Another book was opened, which is the book of life. The dead were judged according to what they had done as recorded in the books. The sea gave up the dead that were in it, and death and Hades gave up the dead that were in them, and each person was judged according to what he had done. Then death and Hades were thrown into the lake of fire. The lake of fire is the second death. If anyone's name was not found written in the book of life, he was thrown into the lake of fire." (Revelation 20:11-15 NIV)*

The details of this event are listed in just a few short sentences, but it is an event that is enormous, unfathomable in size and significance. Can you imagine all those who have ever lived being resurrected and standing before the great throne of God to receive final judgment? Imagine those who ruled so cruelly over the masses, who had power, fame, and riches in this life, seeing the final justice of God when they view those they held as little more than useless slaves receiving an eternal place in God's kingdom while they are sent to eternal punishment. There is no act, no injustice which will go unrecorded, and no prayer that will go unheard.

The scripture above states all the dead will be present at this event. The book of life is also open, so we assume those present at the great white throne judgment are all who have ever lived on the earth, which includes those in Heaven as well as those in Hell. There is further evidence of this by looking at the words that Jesus spoke regarding this event: *"When the son of man shall come in his glory, and all the holy angels with him, then shall he sit upon the throne of his glory: And before him shall be gathered all nations: and he shall separate them one from another, as a shepherd divides his sheep from the goats: and he shall set the sheep on his right hand, but the goats on the left."* *(Matthew 25:31-33KJV)* We can see by his statement that the good as well as the bad, the obedient as well as the disobedient are present before the throne, and he is the one who will divide them, identifying which is which. There is no danger for those who are written in the book of life, and there is no indication their works on earth were what earned them a place in that book. We know their names were written in the book based on their acceptance of Jesus Christ as Lord, the one who purchased their salvation by dying on the cross for their sins, and their faith in Christ alone was the only criteria for having their names written in the book of life. What is the purpose then for this judgment, after all, those who accepted Jesus are in heaven, and those who rejected him are in hell. Doesn't this seem as if the judgment is already passed? It seems as if before God proceeds to a new heaven and new earth, he wants to bring final closure to the present heaven and earth. God is just above all, and he will leave no person without the certainty of why they were recipients of the justice they received. All mankind will stand before him as well as before each other and the real truth will be plainly seen by all. Not only will those who receive eternal punishment in the lake of fire know the reason why, but those who suffered by their hands will see the final judgment of God against those who were so evil against their fellow men. It brings to remembrance the scripture which states, *"For we know him who has said, 'Vengeance belongs to me, I will repay says the Lord'. And again, 'The Lord shall judge his people'."* *(Hebrews 10:30 NKJV)* Jesus also stated regarding the rewards of the righteous: *"And if anyone gives even a cup of cold water to one of these little ones because he is my disciple, I tell you the truth, he will certainly not lose his reward." (Matthew 10:42 NIV)*

The book of Revelation tells us they were all judged according to what they had done. Jesus gives us an insight into the criteria for judgment specifically in Matthew chapter twenty five. From the beginning, God has desired to make us into his image, and while he knows who is who, for us, discerning evil from good, is not always as easy as it seems. Some deeds are evident to all as evil, while other deeds may look good on the surface, but have a very different motive or agenda beneath the surface. God judges according to the motive of the heart where true intentions are hidden. Jesus said out of the heart man speaks; he also said what goes into a man is not what defiles him, but rather, what comes out of him, because what comes out of him proceeds from his heart. God, who knows the very intent and thoughts of our hearts, will judge according to what he sees in our heart. If we look at King David, the word of God states that David had a heart after God, yet David was not a perfect man. Abraham sought after God with his whole heart, and trusted in God, and thus he was called the friend of God, but he was not a perfect man either. God is after our hearts, and once we have given our heart to him, he helps us change the way we behave. We desire to please him, we desire to be like him, and as we surrender to him and begin to walk with him, he begins the process of manifesting his nature in our lives. Instead of a selfish heart, we now have a servant heart. Jesus came to serve, not to be served, and gave his life as a ransom for many. (Mark 10:45) So we see our faith in Christ and our commitment to him is marked by a new attitude, a new heart, one that is evident by the nature to love and serve others. We are truly 'new creations' in Christ.

Jesus referred to this new heart nature as what separates his children from the children of this world. When he spoke concerning the judgment of mankind at the end of the age, he turns to the 'sheep', his children, (which he divided and put on his right hand side), and says: *"Then the King will say to those on his right, 'Come, you who are blessed of my Father; take your inheritance, the kingdom prepared for you since the creation of the world: For I was hungry and you gave me something to eat, I was thirsty and you gave me something to drink, I was a stranger and you invited me in, I needed clothes and you clothed me, I was sick and you looked after me, I was in prison, and you came to visit me.' Then the righteous will answer him, 'Lord, when did we see you hungry and feed you, or thirsty and give you something to drink? When did we see you a stranger and invite you in, or needing clothes and clothe you? When did we see you sick or in prison and go to visit you?' The King will reply, 'I tell you the truth, whatever you did for one of the least of these brothers of mine, you did for me."* *(Matthew 25:34-40 NIV)*

It is clear what was judged here was their hearts, their love for others, not the list of sins they had committed, for in truth, sin comes from a wrong attitude in our heart which leads to rebellious, disobedient, and often deadly actions. Sin is the consequence of a heart which is not right with God. Jesus will judge our heart, our Godly nature, or the lack thereof. If we love, we will have compassion and serve others as Christ did. Remember the scripture states love covers a multitude of sins, in other words, if love rules in our hearts, we will react in a Godly way, not in a selfish way, thus avoiding many ugly sins. Even when we slip up, (as we all do) when we repent and demonstrate it by serving others in love, we have the promise of forgiveness from the Lord. If we say we are sorry for our sins but continue to behave in the same selfish manner, thinking of ourselves first at the cost of others, then we have not truly repented or recognized our hearts were right with God. Our actions reflect the condition of our heart. We are not earning our salvation, for it was freely given by grace to us by what Christ did for us on the cross. It is impossible for us to make atonement for our sins without the cross, for we inevitably fail, therefore we could never make full restitution. Only Jesus can pay the price for ALL our sins and grant us forgiveness and the promise of eternal life. However, having said this, it does not mean the cross is a free "pass" or "get out of jail free" card. It is not a permit or license to sin. The evidence of a true conversion to Christ, a life dedicated to God, is seen in the changed nature or lifestyle of the individual. We no longer want to sin against God, and in the moments of weakness when we succumb to temptation and sin, a great remorse and desire to repent and make things right with God, overwhelms us. The scripture states those in Christ no longer practice sin; in other words, they don't pre-meditate, or plan for sin in their life. Yes, they still may sin, but they don't live to sin, they live to serve God, and it grieves them when they do fall into sin. Why? Because their heart has changed! They are new creatures in Christ, and as such, they WANT to please God by having the right heart, and the actions which correspond, or prove the love for Christ in their hearts.

The opposite is true of those who do not love God, who only love themselves and serve themselves. They do so at the cost of others, for no one is as important as the need THEY have at the moment. They make themselves more important than God; they are their own god. While such people may have moments of compassion, they are ultimately ruled by their own personal agenda or needs, and do not have the nature of the eternal Father, but rather the selfish nature of Satan. Unfortunately, those who reject his constant calling, and choose to serve themselves rather than him will have to eventually pay the price, as we see in the words Jesus spoke to those who were separated as 'goats' to his left: *"Then he will say to those on his left, 'Depart from me, you who are cursed, into the eternal fire prepared for the devil and his angels. For I was hungry and you gave me nothing to eat, I was thirsty and you gave me nothing to drink, I was a stranger and you did not invite me in, I needed clothes and you did not clothe me, I was sick and in prison and you did not look after me.' They also will answer, 'Lord, when did we see you hungry or thirsty or a stranger or needing clothes or sick or in prison, and did not help you?' He will reply, 'I tell you the truth, whatever you did not do for one of the least of these, you did not do for me.' Then they will go away to eternal punishment but the righteous to eternal life." (Matthew 25:34-46 NIV)*

There is a debate among Christians concerning works and grace. In no way does the scripture above state we will receive eternal life due to our good works. This was an issue not understood clearly among the first believers. Paul addressed this issue in many of his letters to the first churches, as seen in his letter to the church in Ephesus: *"For it is by grace you have been saved, through faith, and this not from yourselves, it is the gift of God, not by works, so that no one can boast. For we are God's workmanship, created in Christ Jesus to do good works, which God prepared in advance for us to do." (Ephesians 2:8-10 NIV)* We are saved by God's great grace, his great love, it was not something we could work for or earn on our own; it was his gift to us. However, we also see he saved us for a purpose, to do those things he does, the good works which show forth his love and mercy to mankind. Being saved by grace, we now live to serve. Therefore, we can conclude, as James did, that our faith is made evident by the good deeds which we do. We can't say we are his disciples, and fail to do the things which he did. If we are to indeed be his, we must follow his example. If God is in us, love is in us. John stated that if any man says he loves God but hates his brother, he is a liar, and the love of God is not in him.

Considering this, we can see why Jesus will judge all mankind on that day by what they did or did not do for others, for if the love of God is truly in them, it will manifest itself in

147

good deeds towards others. Remember Jesus said: *"By their fruit you will recognize them. Do people pick grapes from thorn bushes, or figs from thistles? Likewise, every good tree bears good fruit, but a bad tree bears bad fruit. A good tree cannot bear bad fruit, and a bad tree cannot bear good fruit. Every tree that does not bear good fruit is cut down and thrown into the fire. Thus by their fruit you will recognize them."* (Matthew 7:16-20 NIV) What we do for others is a reflection of what we do for the Lord, and it is the measure by which we will be judged when we stand before the Great White Throne Judgment of God. Those who love the Lord will produce good fruit in their lives and those who say they love God, but their actions tell a different story, will be in danger. It appears those who love him and have faithfully served him will see his great justice and mercy, and the punishment extracted on those who persecuted them for their faith in Christ. They will receive their reward for their faith in Christ, as well as for the good works they did in his name. Those who accepted him, but did little in his name will not receive the same reward for their service, however, they win not lose their salvation, for by his grace, by the blood of Christ, and their faith in him, they received that salvation. We are saved by grace not by works, however our good works will not go unrewarded. God's justice is complete, for he knows those who sacrificed and did many loving acts in his name, and he will reward them for their obedience and efforts.

Ultimately, the book of life will determine who enters his kingdom, and who does not. If your name is not found in the book of life, you will not enter into the kingdom God has prepared for those who love him. If you truly love him, you will serve him, and fruit will be produced, thereby your words and your actions will confirm one another. This is the measure for each of us to examine our lives by. We can convince ourselves of anything we want to, but words are cheap, and as we all know, actions speak louder than words. The Bible tells us if we examine ourselves we will not be judged, in other words, if we take stock of our lives, of the deep intents of our own hearts, truthfully and humbly before God, we will repent and get things right with God as we journey in this lifetime. By keeping these scriptures in our hearts and in our minds, his word will help us see when we deviate along the way, and keep us steady on course. We will all be at the Great White Throne Judgment, so let us live our lives for Christ, so we will have nothing to be ashamed about on that day, and we will hear the Lord speak these words to us, "Well done my good and faithful servant".

CHAPTER THIRTEEN

*"Then I saw a new heaven and a new earth, for the first Heaven and the first earth had passed away" (**Revelation 21:1 NIV**)*

As the Bible concludes, it gives us a final revelation; God will create a new heaven and a new earth. It doesn't tell us why he is going to re-do everything, but it does give us some details about this new heaven and earth which he is going to create. There will be no sea, no more great bodies of water that separate us into different countries and nations. We will all be one people, God's people. In Revelation 21:2, John states: *"And I John, saw the holy city, the New Jerusalem, coming down from God out of heaven, prepared as a bride adorned for her husband."* Many believe that this indicates the holy city, which is our dwelling place in heaven, will come down to earth. This is further reinforced by John's statement in verse three; *"And I heard a great voice out of heaven saying, behold, the tabernacle of God is with men, and he will dwell with them, and they shall be his people, and he himself shall be with them, and be their God." (Revelation 21:3 KJV)* God will dwell with man! Now this is not to say that this scripture was not fulfilled when Jesus came to earth and established his Kingdom in the hearts of all who believe, for the Word tells us "And he shall be called Emmanuel", which means God with us. In truth, God has never left us, he has always been with us, and even more so once his plan was "finished" on the Cross. But it doesn't mean there will not be a physical reality as well as the already existing spiritual reality. Isn't this why he created us to begin with? It was always his plan to be with his children, that's why he created us. Why give us a physical, glorified body unless he planned to unite the physical and spiritual realms into one?

He will spend eternity forming us into his likeness and his image. We will be able to see him, to walk with him and talk with him. All the questions we have will be answered. He will teach us all things concerning who he is and what he created us to be. We will learn the mysteries of the universe, of time, and of eternity. God will accomplish what he set out to do!

Wonderful promises follow those first few verses listed above, letting us know how glorious it will be: *"And God shall wipe away all tears from their eyes; and there shall be no more death, neither sorrow, nor crying, neither shall there be any more pain; for the former things are passed away."* *(Revelation 21:4 KJV)* The fear of death will no longer exist! The aches and pains of old age will end! We will not experience sadness, depression or anxiety; there will be no more disease or suffering. What a wonderful existence for mankind! We will finally be able to focus on loving God, and on loving each other. It sounds like heaven on earth, because it is! Throughout man's history we can see a desire within us all to find a utopia, a place of peace and joy. We can see through different cultures and even different religions, how man has always held certain things in common, the struggle between good and evil, the desire for good to triumph, and the desire to find paradise on earth. We have also read of stories about man's search for a "fountain of youth", a search for eternal life. It is amazing this seems to be a fundamental desire instilled in the nature of man. I believe God implanted these "dreams" or desires in mankind to seek and find the ultimate destiny which God has for us. Unfortunately, many try to find the source of these things through their own avenues or inventions, rather than accepting God's road, his plan and design for achieving this. Nevertheless, it is interesting to see this common desire weaving throughout the history of mankind. What man has at times ignorantly been seeking is the very goal of why God created him.

God himself will create a new heaven and earth, and according to scripture, it appears he will bring this new heaven down to the new earth, and live with his creation. John describes the appearance of the New Jerusalem as a jeweled city, like a glistening crown, whose size is 1377 miles in all directions and dimensions. It is an enormous, glorious city where all nations of those who have ever been saved will walk. John then states; *"I saw no temple therein; for the Lord God Almighty and the Lamb are the temple of it. And the city had no need of the sun, neither of the moon, to shine in it; for the glory of God did lighten it, and the Lamb is the light thereof."* *(Revelation 21:22-23 KJV)*

There is no need for a temple to go to worship God, a house for his presence to dwell, because he is there himself; God Almighty lives there with his people! There is no longer a need for a sun or moon to give light, because the brilliance of God's glory gives light to the city eternally, darkness will no longer exist. Those who are redeemed, saved by the Lamb of God from their sins, having their names written in the book of life, will be able to enter this city. The scripture also makes clear those who will not be allowed in this city: *'But the cowardly (fearful), and unbelieving, the vile, the murderers, the sexually immoral (whoremongers), those who practice magic arts (sorcerers), the idolaters, and all liars will have their place in the lake of burning sulfur. This is the second death." (Revelation 21:8 NIV & KJV)*

Only those who have repented of their sins, and accepted the sacrifice that Jesus made on the cross for the forgiveness of those sins, will be able to enter this city. Those who have rejected Christ, who have not repented of their sins, but have continued to live their lives as they please without regard to the consequences, will have been sent to the lake of fire and be eternally separated from God and his holy city. There will be no evil in this city. Why would anyone choose this fate? Who would want to live sixty or so years on this earth doing whatever they pleased, with no thought or regard to God, only to spend eternity suffering for it? What on this earth, or in this life, would be more valuable, more wonderful than what God has planned for us? It would be like someone saying, I'll take a penny now rather than hold out for billions of dollars later. It just doesn't make any sense. The only conclusion I can come to is they just don't understand what is at stake, or the enormous blessing God has in store for them. People often make poor decisions based on their ignorance, but this is your eternal fate we are talking about. It seems this is one issue people should really be searching for information about. As believers, we need to realize the importance of our mission, to inform people of the truth so they can make the right decision. We should live our lives on a daily basis as if we had flashing neon signs saying, "Don't miss heaven, it will be the experience of a lifetime!" How will they know, unless we tell them?

John further states, *"And he showed me a pure river of water of life, clear as crystal, proceeding out of the throne of God and of the Lamb. In the midst of the street of it, (the heavenly city) and on either side of the river, was the tree of life, which bare twelve manner of fruits, and yielded her fruit every month: and the leaves of the tree were for the healing of the nations. And there shall be no more curse: but the throne of God and of the Lamb shall be in it; and his servants shall serve him. And they shall see his face; and his name shall be in their foreheads. And there shall be no night there; and they need no candle, neither light of the sun; for the Lord God giveth them light; and they shall reign forever and ever "* *(Revelation 22:1-5 KJV)*

What a marvelous thing! There will be a beautiful river filled with life for us to drink from, and trees with different life-giving fruits to eat from, that will bring health and strength for eternity to all peoples of all nations who walk in this wondrous city. God will reign forever and ever, and we will live with him in a place which is so beautiful, it is beyond our imagination. We will live in peace, and build loving relationships with all the inhabitants there. We will delight ourselves in the knowledge of the Lord, for he will share his eternal love and knowledge with us. We will learn, sitting at his feet, the mysteries of the universe, and our creative abilities will unfold and develop without restrictions or limits. Imagine the wondrous works of art, the music, and the amazing creations we will achieve, as God instructs us. I imagine for those who like to build and create, the great structures and things they will be able to design. Those who love music, what glorious music they will create, inspired by the very presence of God. Even if we try to imagine it, our imagination will fall far short of what it will actually be like. The best of all will be looking into the eyes of Jesus, to see the profoundly enormous love which flows from those eyes, and to be enveloped in his loving embrace, never to be separated from him. Wow! It is overwhelming to think about, but this will be our eternal home with him; finally we will be with him!

The book of Revelation ends with some statements from the Lord: *"Behold, I come quickly: blessed is he who keeps the sayings of the prophecy of this book."* *(Revelation 22:7); "And behold, I come quickly; and my reward is with me, to give every man according as his work shall be. I am Alpha and Omega, the beginning and the end, the first and the last." (Revelation 22:12-13); "I Jesus have sent mine angel to testify unto you these things in the churches. I am the root and the offspring of David, and the bright and morning star." (Revelation 22:16); "Surely I come quickly." (Revelation 22:20),* to which John replies, *"Amen, Even so, come Lord Jesus."* This is where the word of God ends, with the promise from Jesus Christ of his return, and the response we as a church should have.

This brings me back to the purpose of God in having me write this book. It is a reminder of the Lord's promise to return, to fulfill his plan for us, and what our attitude concerning his return should be. We are to love his return, to desire it above all else, and to be preparing and anticipating the day with great joy, and with diligent preparation. This is the revelation of the Kingdom blueprint, God's eternal plan for man.

When God's Spirit led me to the scripture which said "to those that love his appearing", and then asked me the question, "do they love my appearing?" I had to honestly state, "it doesn't appear so." Do we, the church, as a whole, desire the return of our Lord with our whole heart as we should? Are we making every effort to inform this world of his return? Are we preparing them for this event by preaching the gospel of Jesus Christ to every soul so they might have the opportunity to be a part of his kingdom when he returns? Is there urgency in our hearts to accomplish our mission? Are our hearts overwhelmed with the cares of this world, with the daily events of living, to the point which we have lost our concern for the lost, our zeal for his return? These are questions which each of us must answer on an individual basis, questions which the leaders of the church must ask themselves. It is my prayer for all who read this book to seriously consider these questions, and honestly answer them in prayer before the Lord.

I believe the Lord led me to write this book in order to open our eyes to his greatness, his goodness, his love, his kingdom blueprint or plan and design for us, in order to instill a passion, a burning desire, to become the type of servants he wants us to be, and the world needs us to be. This book is not meant to bring debate over doctrine, or side with any particular point of view, but to help us look more deeply at these issues, maintaining the spiritual purpose of God in revealing the things he has chosen to reveal to us. Don't be side-tracked into doctrinal debate, for only God has the blueprint; only he knows the complete plan. Rather than trying to figure out the dynamics of his plan, we should be focused on what is the message he wants to convey through his plan. In all of the scripture God has attempted to reveal his heart to us. His son Jesus WAS and IS the revelation of his heart. He told us to *"But seek ye first the Kingdom of God and his righteousness, and all these things shall be added unto you."* *(Matthew 6:33KJV)* This is his counsel to all who are seeking answers. We need to seek to be more like Jesus, and to have his kingdom be fully established in our hearts. We don't need to have all the answers we need to have all the fullness of God dwelling in us. Simply put, we need Jesus! Nothing else really matters.

The glorious news is that the Bible ends with assurance from God, Jesus will return! He has revealed his plan for the redemption of mankind, and the eternal destiny of everyone who chooses Jesus Christ. The plan of God in creating us in the beginning comes full circle in the end. The Kingdom blueprint is complete. We are restored to his presence, he has his children home with him; the door can be shut, and a new age can begin. "Even so, come quickly Lord Jesus."